Thail

Islands & Beaches

The Solo Girl's Travel Guide

Alexa West

"If you want to live a life you've never lived, you have to do things you've never done."

Every girl should travel solo at least once in her life.

You don't need a boyfriend, a travel partner or anyone's approval to travel the world. And you don't need a massive bank account or an entire summer off work.

All you need is that wanderlust in your blood and a good book in your hands.

If you've doubted yourself for one moment, remember this:

Millions of girls travel across the globe all by themselves every damn day and you can, too.

You are just as capable, just as smart, and just as brave as the rest of us. You don't need permission- this is your life.

Listen to your gut, follow your heart, and just book that ticket already!

Thailand

Let's Spill Some Tea Real Quick...

Hey, I'm Alexa.

I started The Solo Girl's Travel Guide series not to make tons of money or become famous on Instagram.

I wrote it for my best friend Becky when she came to Thailand for her honeymoon and for my childhood friend Kelsey who was backpacking with her girlfriends around Southeast Asia.

I wrote these guides for my real-life girlfriends all over the world.

All with the goal of showing them the REAL Thailand in a short amount of time on a realistic budget.

A true Thailand vacation should be equal amounts Thai culture, street food, and tan lines. And that's exactly what this guide is!

What this Guide is not...
- An overwhelming deep-dive into Thailand's history
- A 5-hour read with historical dates and ancient facts
- An advertisement for hotels that pay other travel guides to write about them
- A book written by some man who doesn't even live here...

Speaking of men, since the success of The Solo Girl's Travel Guide, I've had many dudes ask me, "Yeah, but why a girl's guide?" Um, because we have tits. And for some reason, that's enough for the world to treat us like toys. We constantly have to ask ourselves questions like....
- Are there drugs in my drink?
- Is that dark alley filled with serial killers?
- Am I going to be kidnapped and sold to the highest bidder?

The answer is usually no, but for us girls, "usually" doesn't cut it. In order to be wild and carefree, we've got to feel 100% safe.

And I've never found a travel guide to take my safety into consideration…so, here we are. Take it from me: a girl who has been traveling solo around the world for almost 10 years straight. I know these countries inside and out.

Go into your vacation knowing that I'm leading you to the BEST, the SAFEST, and the TOTALLY WORTH it spots.

Let your hair down and tell your mom not to worry. I've got you.

Oh, and once you've bought this book…we're officially friends. I'm here if you need me, just write me on Instagram @KohLexi

Is this how you feel about planning the biggest trip of your life?

I can help.

Want to make sure you've planned the best vacation ever?
   ✓   30-minute Skype Itinerary Consultations

Trust me to plan the whole trip for you?
   ✓   Full-on Itinerary Planning with your Bucket List

Don't want to lift a finger?
   ✓   Total Itinerary Planning including Reservations and Flights

Email me at Alexa@TheSoloGirlsTravelGuide.com for rates.

TABLE OF CONTENTS

11

What are We Doing Here?!

Hi My Love,

You might have read my Amazon Best Seller, the original Solo Girl's Travel Guide: Thailand. That baby covers the entire country – north, south and central giving you jungles, city *and* beaches.

But when you've only got room in your suitcase for 20 bikinis, a total deep dive into Thailand's islands and beaches is what you need.

My best travel guide yet, I'm beyond excited to show you how incredible Thailand can be when you've got a little local knowledge.

I went back to the best islands and beaches in Thailand and teamed up with locals to find the most amazing adventures, food, and hotels - specifically with you in mind.

This travel guide is your golden ticket to navigating the most popular travel spots …and also getting off them to discover hidden waterfalls, beaches, and bars - just like a local.

So, as we get into this guide – I want to make a few promises to you:
- ✓ I won't bullshit you and tell you that a beach is awesome if it's not.
- ✓ I will tell you what spots are worth your time - and what spots to skip.
- ✓ And I will make planning this vacation so easy and so fun!!!

Your bags may not be packed, but your vacation officially starts now.

Thailand 101

Welcome to Paradise.

It's no secret that Thailand is home to many of the most beautiful islands and beaches in the world! A visit to Thailand means baby soft white sand, bathwater warm turquoise water, neon green palm trees and an abundance of wildlife both in the water and on land. Thailand is nothing short of magical with Bucket List Goals everywhere you go.

You can scuba dive with Giant Manta rays in the Andaman Sea, stroll with elephants in the jungles of Phuket, rock climb on the limestone cliffs of Railay, and go swimming with Whale Sharks off the coast of Koh Tao. The possibilities are endless…and that's kind of a problem when you have a limited amount of time to see and do it all!

There are nearly 1,445 islands in Thailand and over 2,000 miles of coastline! Choosing which island and beach to explore can be pretty damn overwhelming.

Each region offers a different kind of holiday…yet, a similar holiday. A phenomenon that we in Thailand like to refer to as "Same Same but Different". Meaning, each region is going to offer white sand beaches, coconut shakes underneath the palm trees, snorkeling with colorful fish and all the Pad Thai you can eat. The difference, though? Them vibes!!!

The key to planning the best vacation is to set your travel goals and then budget your time. And that's what I'm here to help you do.

So, let's just do it already!

Fun Thai Fact
"Koh" means "Island" in Thai.

Thailand Weather

When to Visit & Where

Rule of Thumb:

Krabi & Phuket – November -March
Koh Samui – February - July
Koh Chang – November- April
Hua Hin- October -March

Thailand is hot year-round- just some months are stickier than others.

December to April is considered the dry season with temperatures starting at 77°F (25°C) and increasing to about 102°F (35°C) towards the end of the season. Expect around 60% humidity during this season.

Mid-May to September is the rainy season. The temperature will stay pretty steady around 86°F (30°C) but the rain can be unpredictable. Some weeks it will pour and some weeks you won't see more than a couple hours of rain. To save disappointment, expect a couple hours of rain every day in the afternoon during rainy season. Also, humidity can get pretty intense at around 80%.

Wettest Month: September
Hottest Month: April
Most Ideal Time to Visit Thailand: November- February or "High Season"

Note: "High Season" is when Thailand experiences the highest rates of tourism. In other words, this is the season with the best weather and thus, the most visitors taking advantage of the beaches and bars! This also means, however, that prices are higher when it comes to hotels and flights!

So, if your window for your epic Thailand adventure falls outside of High Season- don't worry about it, darling. Take advantage of the lower prices, emptier planes, and embrace the rain! In the end, you'll still get a tan.

Top 10 Thailand Experiences

1- **Elephant Sanctuary & Elephant Park – Phuket**

2- **Get Scuba Certified, Koh Tao**

3- **Tiger Cave Temple, Krabi**

4- **Wat Phra Yai Temple, Koh Samui**

5- **Krabi Sunset Cruises – Railay Beach**

6- **Ang Thong Marine Park Boat Tour – Koh Samui**

7- **Four Island Tour to Emerald Cave, Koh Lanta**

8- **Khao Sok National Park –Khao Lak, Thailand**

9- **Thai Cooking Class, Anywhere!**

10- **Full Moon Party, Koh Phangan**

Top 10 Thailand Beaches

1- **Sunrise Beach, Koh Lipe**

2- **Phra Nang Cave Beach, Railay**

3- **Bottle Beach, Koh Phangan**

4- **Lamai Beach, Koh Samui**

5- **Long Beach, Koh Lanta**

6- **Emerald Cave, Koh Muk**

7- **Coconut Beach, Khao Lak**

8- **Lipa Noi, Koh Samui**

9- **Secret Beach, Koh Samui**

10- **Tri Trang Beach, Phuket**

How to Budget for Thailand

How much money should I bring?
How much will I spend?
What is the least amount I can spend and still see it all?

When it comes to traveling Southeast Asia, there are 3 spending routes you can take:

Budget
Stay in hostels, eat local, take the super convenient minibus, and drink beer from 7-Eleven.

Balanced
Spend the night in a hostel and eat street food one night, then check into a beachfront resort and sip tropical cocktails the next. Or just stay middle of the road the whole way through – not too fancy but comfortable.

Bougie
Infinity pool resorts, private boat tours, and quick flights from one beach to the next.

All 3 of these options are possible, easy and will offer you the trip of a lifetime – as long as you plan it right.

♥	Budget	Balanced	Bougie
Total Per Day	**$30**	**$80**	**$160+**

Daily Expenses

Cost	Price in USD
Thai Street Food	$1.50
Thai Restaurant	$4.00
Hamburger	$8.00
Bottle of Beer	$3.00
Cocktail	$5.00
1 Night in a Hostel	$8.00
1 Night in a Private Room	$30.00
1 Night in a Resort	$110.00 +
Day Tour	$30
1 Hour Flight	$25 - $150
7-Hour Bus	$28

Tips to Spend Less in Thailand

- Visit during "low season" when accommodation and flights are cheaper
- Go to the ATM just once a week – the ATM fees are up to $6 per transaction
- Get a Sim Card and download Grab Taxi
- Drink beer from 7-Eleven or hole in the wall bars, rather than clubs
- Haggle at markets and when street shopping! Start your haggling at half price and work your way from there.
- Avoid Tuk Tuk drivers and fixed-rate taxis
- Eat street food

Your biggest expenses will be

- ✓ Alcohol
- ✓ Partying
- ✓ Organized Island Tours

Everything else can be tweaked to fit your wallet.

Thailand Culture Norms

Girl, you're grown. I know.

But I'll just leave these here in case you're interested....

Thai Do's & Don'ts

Do...

Cover your Shoulders & Knees in the Temples

Modesty is required inside spiritual spaces. Wear a long skirt or buy a Thai shawl to wrap around your waist and/or shoulders when you visit the temples.

Wai

To show respect to your elders, monks, and friends, put your hands in prayer at your chin and give a slight bow of the head- this is a wai. You'll start to love it.

Smile

In tense or unfair situations, argue with a smile. Thais don't like to "lose face" or get embarrassed. You're much more likely to resolve an issue with a smile.

Tip Your Salon Lady

Massages, pedicures, haircuts- these kinds of services definitely deserve a tip. 15-20% should do it.

Don't...

Disrespect the King

This one is a super don't. Thailand loves their king- he was a great man who did a lot for this country. Speaking disrespectfully about him is unheard of.

Show the Bottom of your Feet

In Thailand, feet are seen to be lowly as they are connected to the ground where human suffering occurs. Don't step over people sitting on the ground, don't point the bottom of your feet towards Thais while sitting cross-legged, and *don't don't don't* rest your feet up on a chair or on a seat in the bus.

Touch a Monk

No one- not me, not you, not the Pope- can touch a monk. No handshakes, no selfies and no hugs. Instead, smile and wai.

Wear Bikinis in Public

I know you're on vacation, but Thai People are not. Save your banging bod for the beach or pool and cover up while you walk around town.

Try to Buy anything Illegal

If you go looking for trouble in Thailand, you'll find it. While you might meet travelers with stories of getting high and taking trippy substances, they are all lucky they didn't get caught. Just because drugs are readily available, doesn't mean they're risk-free. Law enforcement is heavily cracking down on partying in Thailand (but often looks the other way for Full Moon Parties). Respect the laws of the country.

Tip Taxis or Servers

I mean, you can if you want to. But typically, Thais don't tip. In some situations, tipping is actually quite awkward.

Activities to Avoid in Thailand

Just because you *can* do it, doesn't mean you *should* do it…

Ping Pong Shows

More traumatizing than entertaining, Ping Pong Shows are where women stick objects and animals inside themselves and perform tricks on stage. If you're out of touch, you may get a rush from how shocking this is to watch. But if you're plugged into reality, you'll likely be horrified for these exploited women who feel that Ping Pong shows are their only opportunity for work. There will be plenty of Thai hawkers inviting you Ping Pong shows while you walk around touristy areas- just ignore them and walk along. Purchasing a ticket is perpetuating a disgusting industry.

Tattoos of Buddha

Buddha is sacred in these parts. So much so, that in neighboring Myanmar, a backpacker was jailed for having a tattoo of Buddha. That is quite unlikely to happen to you in Thailand, but it goes to show how disrespectful it is.

Riding Elephants

What may seem like a 'Bucket List' activity is actually an industry bred out of animal cruelty and torture. Instead of riding elephants, find an elephant sanctuary that allows you to feed, trek and bathe in the river with elephants rescued from the circus, work camps and elephant riding tourist centers around Thailand.

Tiger Temples

Those cute baby tigers that you're about to take a photo with…do you ever wonder where they come from? Tigers are essentially farmed, taken from their mothers at 2 weeks old, and given to tourists to bottle feed. And that's only the beginning…

Some Tips Before You Go!

Beer, Wine & Alcohol Sale Times
Alcohol is sold between 11am-2pm & 5pm-11pm. This goes for all supermarkets and convenient stores. However, if you can find a little Mom & Pop shop- they'll hook you up 24/7.

The Tour Companies actually have Great Deals
Walking around any tourist area in Thailand, you'll see plenty of tour companies with books of jungle treks and floating market tours. For day trips, these companies are pros at giving you great experiences for great prices. As far as multi-day trips, you'll save a couple bucks by planning those on your own.

Toasties
Curry is good but 7-11 Toasties are better. Grab one of these sandwiches from the fridge section of 7-11 and hand it to the 7/11 staff who will cook it for you. The ham and cheese croissant is my favorite! Warning: these treats are addictive!

Bumble
Find a sightseeing partner with another traveler or link up with a local who knows all the best spots in the city. This is a very date-friendly country. Just avoid Tinder…it's more popular for illicit dating…

Ask for "No Sugar"
Thai's love processed sugar. They put it in fresh fruit smoothies, coffee, and even will scoop a tablespoon into your soup. I find myself asking for no sugar nearly every time I order something – no matter what it is. If you like your food fresh, don't feel weird doing the same.

Cheap Flights with Air Asia
When flying in and around Thailand, check out Air Asia. Cheap, convenient and safe – just know that you'll have to pay extra to check a bag.

Carry Passport Photos
If you're country hopping, get cheap passport photos made in Thailand and carry them around in your wallet. This will save you time and money during border crossings.

Download Local Apps
This city is connected to some awesome apps that will make your trip a lot easier and a lot cheaper if you use them!

❖ **Grab Taxi.** Grab Taxi is like Uber but tends to be cheaper and have more cars available. Some Grabs are actual Taxis, and some are private cars. You can pay cash on the taxi meter or pay by card

❖ **Eatigo.** This city-wide food app offers insane food deals up to 50% off all around the city. Why not plan your day around food?

❖ **Line.** Most Thai locals use Line as their messenger app in place of WhatsApp. You can make calls and text with fun little stickers on wifi.

Keep in Mind
ATMs in Thailand spit out your money first and your card second, resulting in many a forgotten card.

Okay enough of all that. Let's get to the fun stuff!

Section 1:

The Andaman Sea of Thailand

Region #1

The Andaman Sea

 Easy Term: The West Coast

 Includes:
- ✓ Phuket
- ✓ Krabi
- ✓ Koh Phi Phi
- ✓ Koh Chang
- ✓ Koh Lanta
- ✓ Koh Lipe
- ✓ Khao Lak
- ✓ Phrang Nga Bay

 Best for...
- • Island-hopping, secret beaches & scooter adventures

 Known for...
- • Scuba diving, snorkeling, and rock climbing

 Best time to Visit: November - March

Chapter 1: Phuket

Ah, Phuket. It's like that loud, obnoxious acquaintance from high school whose Dad owned the local Pizza Hut franchise, so you'd let him tag along on the weekends knowing that you could get free pizza when you were drunk, but if you didn't plan on drinking then you would go out of your way to avoid their calls on a Saturday night.

Does that analogy make sense or is it just me?

Listen, if you know me or are familiar with my books at all…you know that I'm not a huge fan of Phuket. It's crowded, overpriced, and doesn't represent the tropical paradise you've been dreaming of.

BUT from an island & beaches perspective, there are some upsides.
✓   Phuket's International Airport is an easy hub to fly into.
✓   Flights to the rest of the country are convenient.
✓   The Elephant Sanctuaries are the only ethical ones in the south.
✓   And there's a Hooters. I love fried pickles.

So, no need to spend a week here. Spend a couple days and then escape to a nearby island where you can experience the real Thailand.

While you're here, however, I'll navigate you around the tourist landmines and direct you to the most enjoyable spots on the island while getting the most bang for your buck.

I said I'd never write a Phuket chapter…but here I am. I'm going to give you guys the basics from hotels and transportation to the best beaches – but just enough to spend a day or two. After that, run for your lives.

Area Breakdown

Phuket is the biggest island in Thailand, 40 miles from north to south, and 21 miles from east to west. There are 17 districts – but knowing about each district will do absolutely nothing for planning your trip.

Instead, we're going to break the island up into 4 tourist sections:

The Northwest

Home to Phuket's international airport, Northwest Phuket is perhaps the least chaotic with more upscale resorts and Sririnat National Park. You'll find some of the best beaches up here; beaches that haven't *yet* been spoiled by massive hordes of tourists. Some of the most notable beaches in the north include Bang Thao, Banana Beach, Laem Sing, Mai Khao, Bang Thao, Nai Thon and Nai Yang, and Surin.

Patong and the Southwest

Most tourists that visit Phuket stay in this area. Patong is known as the party capitol of Asia – with tons of western restaurants, shopping everywhere and nightlife that never quits. However, what most people don't know is that you can easily escape this Patong party area and stay at a nearby beach such as Kamala, Karon, Kata, Kata Noi.

Phuket Town

I'm not really sure why anyone stays here to be honest, and so I won't be writing much about it. Phuket Town is just a...town. A typical Thai town with a couple night markets, some malls and cafes. If you're catching a morning ferry, I suppose you could stay in Phuket Town which is home to Rassada Pier – or you can just take a taxi from a more peaceful spot.

Rawai

Rawai encompasses the southeast chunk of Phuket that starts inland and then jets off onto a rocky peninsula called Promthep Cape. Life is a bit quieter down here with some scenic beaches and viewpoints – but not much in terms of socializing or partying.

The Beaches of Phuket

Okay so! When you visit Phuket, there is a list of beaches that local tour shops always recommend.

The funny part is, many of these locals have never visited these beaches themselves or they visited once 5 years ago and haven't been back. It's sounds strange, but that's just how island life goes.

So, when you ask for beach recommendations, you'll get a go-to list of beaches that are easy to recommend and when you ask, "Is it beautiful" they will say, "Oh yes, it's so beautiful" because they DGAF.

You ain't got time for the bullshit, babe. Now, I'm going to tell you what's really up with these beaches.

Which are worth a visit?
Which are worth skipping?
PLUS I'll tell you a few beaches that are not on the go-to tourist list.

The Northwest

Mi Khao Beach

Oddly enough, right next door to Phuket Airport is one of the emptiest beaches in Phuket! We're talking deserted island empty in some spots along this 7-mile beach. Translating into "wood sand", the sand is grainy here instead of powdery soft and the waves can be a bit intense in some spots. Walk along until you find calm waters and some shade.

Nai Yang Beach

Part of Sritinat National Park, the jungle, shore and waters of Nai Yang Beach are totally protected! White sand, gorgeous water. You could spend all day here. Just bring snacks and water with you. There aren't many of shops nearby.

Bangtao Beach

This 4-mile stretch of beach is the lined with fancy resorts which has prompted markets and restaurants to pop up nearby. The beach itself has beautiful white sand and water that is perfect for swimming, but from the water looking in – it's all lounge chairs, beach beverage shacks, and hawkers. With so much space however, it doesn't feel to invasive on your beach day.

Banana Beach

Relatively off the beaten path, Banana Beach – known to the locals as Hat Hin Kluay – is gorgeous and serene. Marked only by a wooden sign nailed to a tree, you have to be looking for this beach in order to find it. Banana Beach is slowly making its way onto the tourist radar, so you'll find a few massage ladies and some beverage stands on the perimeter of the shore – but not enough to ruin the experience.

Pro Tip

May to November is the best time swim here. Outside of this window, the water gets a bit murk.

Nai Thon Beach

Often referred to as the "Imperfect Perfect Beach", Nai Thon is that postcard beach you've been dreaming. Some days the sand is pink and some days the sand is white – it all depends on the season. No matter when you come, you can enjoy this quiet retreat from the tourist path!

Restaurants and drinks nearby are relatively expensive thanks to the nearby upscale villas and resorts – but these prices also weed out the crowds. Just bring snacks and you're good.

Surin

In terms of beauty, Surin does have white sand and small surf waves – but it's relatively crowded and surrounded by villas that have bulldozed most of the jungle. Not exactly scenic but an okay vacation beach if you're looking to stay in an area with lots of food and hotel options.

Patong and the Southwest

Patong Beach

If hell had a beach, this would be it. Patong Beach is popular for Russians wearing banana hammocks, families with young children and Thai hawkers trying to sell you shit that you would never need in a thousand lifetimes. Go to the very north end of Patong Beach and you'll find a quieter strip with lots of toe-in-the-sand Thai restaurants. The area itself is broken down by 1st, 2nd, and 3rd street which head from the water inland. Each street is a maze of shopping, restaurant, and hotel. It's madness and does not represent Thailand – but nonetheless, it's an interesting sight to see.

Paradise Beach

With a Miami feel, Paradise Beach is a private Beach Club where sexy people go to mingle and lounge on beachfront day beds during the day – and listen to live DJs and party at night. The catch? Nothing is free – but not ridiculously expensive either.

Entrance is 200 baht and **lounge beds are 300 baht.** Paradise Beach *does* offer a Free Round-Trip Shuttle Bus from Patong Beach 4x per day. Check them out on Facebook for exact times and locations.

Paradise Beach is also home to the **Full Moon & Half Moon Party.**
1000 Baht for 1 bucket or 2 beers OR 1500 baht for 2 buckets and a Paradise Beach Tank Top. Entrance is included!

Kamala Beach

Kamala Beach is just to the North of Patong Beach. It's amazing how a 10-minute drive can offer such a different scene. The beach is big and beautiful with white sand and blue water. It does draw a crowd – but a tolerable crowd. The area has cool with a mix of Thai and Western restaurants, plus a Wednesday and Friday night markets, and a weekly Saturday market.

Tri Trang Beach

White powdery sand and blue sparkling water, this is best beach in this area. Tri Trang Beach is secluded down a steep hill and has only one resort on the shore - Tri Trang Beach Resort. The beach feels like a secret, with only a few Russian families splashing about or having a cold beer at their beach bar.

Karon Beach

This beach is a cool area – rather than a paradise found. The street lining Karon Beach has plenty of cool shops and restaurants. The beach itself is the 3rd longest on the island with plenty of space for your beach towel. It's more comfortable than it is spectacular.

Kata Beach

A tolerable balance between chaos and peace – Kata Beach offers some activities like parasailing and massages on the beach, and also some spots where you can seclude yourself and spend a day in the sun with your book. The neighborhood surrounding is similar – and not far from – Karon beach, as well.

Kata Noi Beach

In my opinion, Kata Noi is the second-best beach in the Patong area. It's a tiny beach at the very end of the Patong area. It's quite with just a couple beach shacks offering food and drink. The surrounding hillside is gorgeous and has some pretty swanky villas to gawk at.

Rawai

Nai Harn Beach

The most popular beach in Rawai! Why? Because its big and the water is decent for swimming…at least, I suspect that's why. The sand is bright orange and the beach get super crowded in high season with humans and umbrellas. Meh.

Ao Sane Beach

An interesting little beach with large rocks that create little pools to sit in, Ao Sane is a pleasant stop over. There are corals here for snorkeling. They've been largely destroyed so not too colorful, but you can still see a few schools of fish here.

Friendship Beach

This is a beautiful private beach owned by Friendship Beach Resort. To visit, you don't have to stay here but you do have to be a paying customer – 300 baht per person. Come for lunch or order a couple of beers and lounge on the white sand and take a dip in the calm, shallow waters.

Chalong Bay

More of a boat port than a beach – Chalong Bay is home to the majority of the dive shops which offer dive courses and snorkeling trips around the island.

Accommodation in Phuket

Northwest

Coriacea Boutique Resort $$

Flying into Phuket for one day and then heading for Krabi? This hotel is my pick for a quick stop over if you plan on taking road transport to Krabi. Coriacea Boutique Resort is a cute little resort situated right across from Mai Khao Beach – one of the best kept beaches in Phuket – and is located at the top of Phuket Island, making an easy public bus ride or private taxi journey to Krabi the next day. Breakfast is plenty, bikes are free, and the staff go above and beyond with true Thai hospitality.

Starts at: $60 USD / 200 THB
Where: Mai Khao Beach
Address: 89/2 Soi Mai Khao 6, Moo 4, T.Maikhao

Naiyang Park Resort $$

Traditional Thailand village vibes with modern amenities next to the most beautiful public beach in Phuket – if you weren't sure what to do with your extra days in Phuket, here is the answer, babe! You'll be tucked into a spacious Thai cottage with wooden floors and a cozy bed. Throw your bags down and kick your feet up on your balcony surrounded by Thai jungle with a wooden walkway that lights up at night, leading you towards the massive pool and quaint restaurant. The beach is a just quick 3-minute walk from the resort and the airport is a 5-minute drive. You're all set.

Starts at: $100 USD / 3500 THB
Where: Nai Yang Beach
Address: 34/5 Tambon Sakoo, Thalang

Andaman White Beach Resort $$$

Situated on a private beach in the middle on the Sririnat National Park, here is where you come to get your zen on. This beach is one of the cleanest, most private and pristine beaches you find in Phuket with soft white sand and crystal-clear water. Best of all...no crowds! Each room gives you a stunning view of the water, as does the pool and restaurant on site. Great pizza, fabulous happy hour, and free afternoon fruit. Just a 10-minute walk into town and 15-mintues from Phuket Airport, this is the perfect place to start or end your Thailand trip.

Starts at: $259 USD / 8560 THB
Where: Between Banana Beach and Nai Thon Beach
Address: 28/4 Moo 4, Tambon Sakoo, Thalang District

Anantara Layan Phuket Resort $$$

Truly, the best resort in Phuket is Anantara Layan located on a private white sand beach at the entrance of Sririnat National Park. This resort is the epitome of luxury, fit for a queen on vacation! Every amenity is top notch and the service is impeccable. Never underestimate attention to detail; the lavender spray for your pillow at night, the beach bags for your trip to the beach, kayaks for exploring and high-quality healthy breakfasts with a mimosa station leaves you feeling pampered and refreshed. This is what you came to Thailand for.

Starts at: $350 USD / 11500 THB
Where: Sririnat National Park
Address: 168 Moo 6, Layan Beach Soi 4, Cherngtalay

Patong

Lub D Hostel $

Jaw dropper. There's no other hostel on this planet that has a Muay Thai gym in the lobby and an independent tattoo shop behind reception. This place is massive and packed with every Thai activity that you need to check off your bucket list. Every day, they offer free events like Muay Thai Lessons, cooking classes, Thai language classes, beach excursions...it's seriously incredible. They have a pool, a restaurant and a coworking space all tucked inside this spacious hostel AND it's only a 3-minute walk to the beach.

Style: Dorms and Privates
Starts at: $18 USD / 600 THB
Where: Patong Beach
Address: 5/5 Sawatdirak Rd, Tambon Patong, Amphoe Kathu

Bodega Resort $

When you come to Bodega, you don't have to worry about making friends – they are built in. Bodega Staff are essentially sexy camp counselors who are always up to weird antics and rope you into joining. Pool days, pub crawls, and drinking games make it easiest for even the shyest of solo travelers to wind up with a crew. When the madness is over, collapse into the most heavenly dorm beds you'll find in all of Thailand!!! In the morning, their on-site restaurant will be waiting to stuff you full with a big ass breakfast.

Bodega Tip: Want to be social but have some privacy at the same time? Bodega's private rooms have bathtubs and English TV channels! Be rowdy when you please and then get in some "me" time.

Style: Dorms and Privates
Starts at: $12 USD / 440 THB
Where: 3rd Street – a 5-minute walk to the night markets
Address: 5/5 Sawatdirak Rd, Tambon Patong, Amphoe Kathu

Pro Tip

If you are hosteling it up in Phuket, I suggest splitting half the time between Bodega and Lub D – they both offer amazingly different vibes.

Patong Terrace Boutique Hotel $$

When you want to be alone but not invisible - staying in a small boutique hotel is the way to go. No face goes unnoticed here, but you still have plenty of privacy. The manager, Peter, works with each guest to help you customize the perfect tour of Phuket. See the Big Buddha, go to the best beaches, and even throw a Muay Thai Match in the mix. He'll help you set it all up over breakfast! Afterwards, come home and collapse. The rooms are simple and best for budget travelers - but there are English channels on TV and rain showers with proper water pressure to wash your hair! **Ps.** Try the homemade apple pie with a fresh coffee. To die for.

Style: Privates
Starts at: $30 USD / 1000 THB
Where: 5 Minute-Walk from Patong Beach
Address: 209/12-13 Rat-U-Thit Rd., Patong

The Charm Resort Phuket $$$

The rooftop infinity pool overlooking the ocean and the sky bar that lights up at night are the main selling points for this lux hotel. The rooms are everything you could want and more. If you plan to hang at your hotel with a few explorations to the beach – this is all you need. Head up: if night markets were on your to-do list, plan on spending $10-$20 round trip getting there – or walking 20 minutes each way. The Charm Resort is located on the north end of Patong Beach.

Starts at: $100 USD / 9500 THB
Where: 5 Minute-Walk from Patong Beach
Address: 212 Thaweewong Road, Kathu

Burasari Phuket $$$

Pool or beach? You decide. Burasari Phuket has one of the biggest hotel pools in the city *and* is just a 5-minute walk to the sands of Patong Beach. The hotel is new and the attention to detail is totally Instagram-worthy. From the generous breakfast spread to the enthusiasm of the English-speaking staff, it's hard to find a fault in this ultra-comfortable home away from home.

Starts at: $120 USD / 4000 THB
Where: 5 Minute-Walk from Patong Beach
Address: 18/110 Ruamjai Road, Tambon Patong

Glam Habitat Hotel $$$

The name says it all, queen. Glam Habitat Hotel feels like the set of Sex and The City – with concrete architecture, grassy rooftop gardens, high-tech rooms, a brand-new gym and staff that go the extra mile to make sure you're comfortable. Rooms are stocked with all the papering amenities you need: lush robes, cozy slippers, a lighting makeup mirror…and if you shell out an extra penny, you can slip into the pool from your balcony. The bar here is a must-visit, with handcrafted cocktails (a hard find in this city).

Starts at: $160 USD / 5300 THB
Where: 5 Minute walk to Kamala Beach
Address: 112/39 M.3 Kamala Rd., Kamala, Kathu District

Amari Phuket $$$$

Stay in the Patong area without feeling like you're in Patong. Amari Hotel is uniquely built within the cliffside of Patong, surrounded by jungle with unobstructed views of the ocean. Whether you're in your luxury room or the glittering infinity pool, all you see is beauty. You're just a 15-minute walk to Patong Beach and a 20-minute walk to the night markets and nightlife – or take the daily shuttle into town. Wanna stay in? The clubhouse Happy Hour from 5:30-6:30 offers unlimited drinks and finger food - free of charge. Plus, this is a great way to meet some people! Treat yo'self.

Starts at: $180 USD / 6000 THB
Where: 5-minute walk to Patong Beach
Address: 2 Meun-Ngern Road, Kathu

Karon & Kata

Doolay Beachfront Hostel $

Just a few steps to Karon Beach and a quick 5-minute walk to Kata Beach – Doolay Hostel is the perfect balance between scenic and social. When you're not on the beach, have a lazy day in the common area where there are two big couches and a flat screen. Around sunset, travelers usually have a few beers with the balcony and then head out together in search of a little nightlife. Making friends here is easy.

Starts at: $14 USD / 460 THB
Where: 1-minute walk to Karon Beach
Address: 164 Karon Road Tambon Karon

Allstar Guesthouse $

The perfect place to throw your bags down and go exploring. Allstar Guesthouse is simple, spacious, and clean with friendly hosts who are hands-on in helping you plan your day. They direct you towards the beach, the markets, and give you all the food recommendations. Plus, they'll arrange hotel shuttles, ferry transfers, and around-town taxis – taking so much stress off of you and your plans!

Starts at: $27 USD / 2800 THB
Where: 5-minute walk to Karon Beach
Address: 514/13 Patak Road, 83100 Karon Beach

Sugar Ohana Poshtel $$

Traveling with your laptop and want to get some work done? Or simply want to hang out with some coffee café vibes? This clean and cozy poshtel near Kata Noi beach is a sophisticated oasis with complimentary breakfast, beach bag, and beach towel. The staff are really helpful and will show you where you can catch the local bus into Phuket Town for just 40 baht. Need to arrange an airport or ferry transfer? They do that, too, and for some of the cheapest prices around.

Starts at: $55 USD / 1900 THB
Where: 15-minute walk to both Karon & Kata Beach
Address: 88/5 Kata Road, Karon, Phuket, 83100

Jazz U Garden Resort $$$

Solo ladies who want to make some travel friends – here's your spot. The super unique garden pool with scattered day beds creates a naturally social atmosphere, and on top of that, there are a few social activities during the week including with live jazz bands and Latin dancing on Monday, Tuesday, and Friday. Travelers of all ages stay here, compared to hostels where you usually get the younger crowd!

Starts at: $55 USD / 1900 THB
Where: 5-minute walk to both Kata Beach and 10-minutes to Karon Beach
Address: 18/7 Moo 2, Katekwan Rd., T.Karon

The Village Resort & Spa $$$

Who doesn't love a swim-up pool bar? Reasonable beer and cocktail prices plus a 4:00-6:00 pm happy hour is enough to keep you in your swimsuit all day long. Each tropical villa has its own little balcony surrounded by enough greenery to make you feel like you aren't in the city any more. You are 10 minutes to Karon Beach and 10 minutes to Kata Beach – The Village Resort really the best of all worlds when you've got a couple days to spend in Phuket.

Starts at: $100 USD / 3250 THB
Where: 10-minute walk to Karon & Kata Beach
Address: 566/1 Patak Road, Karon Beach

Centara Grand Beach Resort Phuket $$$

Where beachfront actually means beachfront, Centara Grand offers the opportunity to slip out of the pool and step straight onto Karon Beach – but you might not want to leave any of the THREE pools with waterslides, waterfalls, a lazy river and shallow tanning surfaces. There's a gym, a spa, and every room comes with a bathtub. Not to mention, waking up to views of the ocean is definitely #VacationGoals. The only down-side…children may invade your space on occasion. This hotel is family-friendly so just perfect your 'floating away gracefully' skills.

Starts at: $230 USD / 7500 THB
Where: Beachfront on Karon Beach
Address: 683 Patak Road, Muang, 83100 Karon Beach

Rawai

Sea Safari Glamping $$

Glamping on the beach, anyone? Wake up to views of the water in your tent equipped with an electric fan, cozy bed and private bathroom. While the beach isn't great for swimming, the pool is perfect. There's Sea Safari Restaurant next door and a massage place to give you a rub down on the beach. You can rent kayaks for 100 baht a day or play board games with fellow travelers. Outside of that, all there's left to do is nothing. Just unwind and take it easy.

Starts at: $52 USD / 1750 THB
Where: Beachfront on Karon Beach
Address: Moo 5, Wiset Road, Sunrise Beach 1, Phuket, 83150 Rawai Beach

…yea that's it for Rawai. Rawai is a fun place for a day trip but I don't recommend staying over here.

Smaller Islands Nearby

The Naka Island $$$

A tiny island off the coast of Phuket in Phra Nang Bay, Naka Island IS the postcard destination you've been looking for...the only question is, can you afford it?

This small island has just one resort – and it is fancy! Ranging from $350 - $700 USD per night, The Naka Island submerges you in total luxury with tropical villas and celebrity service. With very few people visiting the island, the island has managed to maintain its colorful corals, pristine beaches, and gorgeous jungle – all for you.

Once you get sick of the 5-star infinity pool resort, don't worry – there's Naka Spa, COMO Beach Club, Z Bar and a couple local shacks to take advantage of. You can also go on snorkeling trips or kayaking adventures.

To get there, you'll head to Ao Po Grand Marina on the Northeast Peninsula of Phuket. The Naka Yai will have arranged a boat for you ahead of time which will be waiting to pick you up.

Starts at: $350 USD / 11500THB
Where: Naka Yai

Where to Eat in Phuket

Phuket is a night market island! The best meals you will have will be at a night market – and you can find the full list in the 'Markets & Shopping' section below.

But if you want to grab a few quick bites, here are the *few* places I recommend…

Patong & the South

Surf House Patong Beach & Kata Beach

Surf House is both a fabulous place to grab a juicy western burger or a full on American breakfast AND a place to learn how to surf for around 1000 baht per hour. Surf House has one of those mechanical wave creators that creates a steady wave to surf. If surfing isn't your thing, that's okay – it's just as fun to watch people taking turns surfing and faceplanting.

Open: 9:30am- Midnight
Where: Patong Beach
Address: 151 Thawewong Rd, Tambon Patong

&

Open: 9:30am- Midnight
Where: Kata Beach
Address: 4 Pakbang Road Kata Beach Karon

DooDee

For your first time trying true Asian/Thai food in Thailand, I recommend DooDee for a quick lunch. DooDee 1 serves Thai Food and DooDee 2 serves Cantonese/ Vietnamese soups. They are directly next to each other and are both a must-visit for clean and tasty dishes. Portions are hefty and prices are cheap. The place is always packed – which is always a good sign!

Open: 6:00 am-3:00am
Where: Patong – 3rd street
Address: 74/1 Phangmuang Sai Kor

Cantina

Menu items like "Big Ass Breakfast" and a burger called "Bacon Bacon Bacon" might give you an idea what La Cantina is all about. When you're so hungry that you're hangry – this is where you come to sort your life out. Decisions are easy and portions are huge. Plus, there are vegetarian options and authentic Thai food for your picky friends…

Open: 7:00am-9:00pm
Where: Attached to Bodega Resort
Address: 1, 1 Sirirat Rd, Tambon Patong

Highlights & Lowlights in Phuket

Highlights

The Big Buddha

Made mostly of Burmese White Jade Marble, this gorgeous Buddha gracefully sits 45 meters tall at the top of a mountain overlooking Kata Beach. Drive up to pay your respects and then take in the stunning 360-degree views of Phuket. Just remember to bring something to cover your shoulders and knees.

I recommend adding this Big Buddha visit into a day of beach hopping....

Beach Hopping
Thought I was going to leave you hanging on that one?

Make the most of your time in Phuket and hire a driver to take you to the beaches of your choosing. Usually, the way it works is like this: you hire a driver for 3/4/5 hours and give him 4-5 destinations you'd like to go. He drops you off and patiently waits for you to do your thang. You don't have to fit all these spots in. If you're having a great time at one beach, stay there!

The most logical way to do this is to cut the island in half, and either do the northern beaches or the southern beaches.

You can approach any tourist kiosk and tell them you want a private beach tour. BUT if you are in the Patong area, head over to Patong Terrace Boutique Hotel in the morning and tell them I sent you. You can get a 4-hour tour for 900 baht with drivers who have great track record.

Promthep Cape

The rocky peninsula that jets out of Phuket's Southeast corner is called Promthep Cape. The road leading here is well paved. This is where the majority of tourists stop to take photos or visit the nearby golden elephant lighthouse. Not you, though! Keep going! Throw on a pair of sneakers and take a leisurely hike down the little staircase heading into nature and follow the red dirt path (you'll see it, I promise). This path will lead you to the very tip of the cape. The first section of the path is surrounded by tall jungle and the other half - stunning views of the water and rocky shores below. Once you reach the tip of the cape, you've got a gorgeous 180-degree view of pure island beauty.

Pro Tip

Go in the morning to beat the crowds (they get massive here) or get down to the tip of the cape for sunset!

Soi Dog Foundation

In Thailand, animal rights aren't recognized by locals. This means few dogs are properly cared for, vaccinated, and most definitely, are not neutered. In turn, this has led to Thailand's massive "Soi Dog" or "Street Dog" population. The Soi Dog foundation is a street dog and cat rescue mission, rehabilitation facility and educational awareness center that offers volunteering opportunities to anyone who has a soft spot for these creatures.

You can volunteer by socializing with dogs or cats, to ready them to be fostered or adopted. You can also be a "Flight Volunteer" which means chaperoning a dog or cat back home, on their way to be adopted in the west. While the foundation prefers that volunteers stay for a few weeks at a time, you can pay the foundation a visit (no booking ahead needed) at the times found on their website.

Contact: SoiDog.org
Where: Mi Khao Beach
Address: 167/9 Moo 4, Soi Mai Khao 10, Tambon Mai Khao

Phuket Elephant Sanctuary & Elephant Park

Phuket Elephant Sanctuary – home to 7 rescued elephants.

When it comes to picking an ethical elephant sanctuary, you've got to be fastidious with your research. There are many "elephant sanctuaries" that hide under the word "sanctuary" while still offering elephant rides and practicing animal abuse at their camp – this happens all around Thailand.

Recently, however, **two** true elephant sanctuaries have opened up in Phuket. They each operate a bit differently. Think of **Phuket Elephant Sanctuary as a private school** with wonderful education for us humans and stimulating playtime facilities for the elephants. Think of **Phuket Elephant Park as a Montessori School** where the elephants are in charge and make their own schedules.

Both sanctuaries are essentially **retirement homes for elephants** that have spent their whole lives doing back-breaking work like tourists rides and logging down here in the south.

At Phuket Elephant Sanctuary, your day will start with a quick educational class on elephant behavior and the plight of Asian elephants in the region. Then you'll change into traditional Karen (Burmese Hill Tribe) clothing and spend the day roaming with and feeding the elephants.

How Much: 2,500 baht for a Half Day
Includes: Lunch & Hotel Pick-up
Also Offered: Full days, overnight stays, and volunteering opportunities.

At Phuket Elephant Park is also a retirement home for elephants, where the elephants roam totally chain-free, wandering their natural habitat freely. At Phuket Elephant Park, plan to spend the day just hanging out with the elephants, walking with the herd, watching them in explore and feeding them when they decide they're hungry.

How Much: 3,000 baht for a half day
Includes: Pick up from your Hotel

Good to Know

There are two schools of thought on mud-baths: while the elephants seem to enjoy the mud baths and river, some camps prefer not to keep their elephants on a schedule. Neither of these parks offer elephant bathing.

Not So fun Thai Fact

At the start of the 20th century Thailand had over 100,000 Asian elephants. Today, it's estimated that there are just around 4,000 elephants left, of which just 1,500 live in the wild.

Want to help those numbers increase? Say no to elephant riding establishments. Support elephant sanctuaries.

Muay Thai Boxing Camps

All year round, people come from every corner of the planet to train Muay Thai in Phuket. Girls, guys, celebrities (I've got stories) – every human of every fitness level can come and train. Your goal can be to get in shape or to eventually participate in a real boxing match in a real stadium. Come for a single drop in class for around $10 USD or stay for a few weeks or months – Muay Thai Camps offer accommodation in their longer-term training packages.

Some of the more popular camps to check out:

- Tiger Muay Thai
- Sinbi Muay Thai
- Kinkga Supa Muay Thai
-

Low Lights

The Phi Phi Island Tour

Every tour office really pushes the Phi Phi Island Tour. What they don't tell you is that you're on a boat for 8 hours. Yep. 4 hours each way inside of a bumpy speed boat. Once you get to Phi Phi, the tour simply lets you lose for a few hours and then you climb back aboard for another 4 hours.

A Better Idea: Go to Phi Phi on your own. Stay 1 or 2 nights, and then come back to Phuket.

Markets & Shopping

Street Shopping

In terms of clothing, everywhere you walk in Patong – you'll find a
clothing shop selling bathing suits, dresses, tank tops with cheeky
sayings and workout gear that are surprisingly great quality knockoffs
of Nike, Under Armour and Adidas. You can also find jewelry,
speakers, headphones....knives. Whatever you want.

Phuket Weekend Market / Naka Market

The biggest market in Phuket and one of the biggest markets in all of
Thailand – there is so much to buy and taste that it's almost
overwhelming! Every food under the sun, plus leather bags, vintage
clothes, tradition Thai oils...you name it, they've got it.

Where: Phuket Town near Central Festival
When: Saturday & Sunday 4:00 pm – 9:00 pm

Pro Tip

If you see something you like, buy it now. The "I'll come back later"
attitude will fail you in the massive maze.

Karon Temple Market

The only market that's worth planning your day around is Karon
Market. You'll find the same genre of clothing and food here that you
would in other markets (beachwear and funny tank tops) but with
more of a variety. Even better news, Karon Market has been dubbed
"street food safe" – meaning that the street food here is some of the
freshest and so, your odds of getting a sour stomach at few! There's
never a guarantee, but this is the closest thing to it.

Where: Karon Beach - 500 meters from the Karon Circle
When: Tuesday and Friday 4:00 pm-10:00 pm

Malin Plaza Patong

Perhaps the best night market in terms of freshness and options,
Malin Plaza Patong is a great place to try some local cuisine. You'll
find stall after stall of freshly caught fish – all of which are labeled
with a clear price (usually 200 baht per), along with crab, oysters and
langoustines. Pick what you'd like, and the chefs will grill them up for
you on the spot. You'll also find plenty of fruit, fried rice stands, and

even a crocodile stand. There are picnic style tables where you can sit down and order a cold beer to go with your piping hot Thai food.

Where: South end of Patong Beach – Near Duangjitt Resort
When: Daily 2:00pm – 12:00am

Patong OTOP Shopping Paradise

More food and less shopping, actually. OTOP comes alive at night with brightly lit food stands offering everything from traditional stir-fried Thai dishes to drunk kebabs! There are tables all around. Have a seat, eat, and then explore the handful of elephant pant and purse shops that line the plaza.

Where: Patong Beach – Opposite of Hooters
When: Daily 5:00pm – 12:00am

Phuket Sunday Street Market

If you're okay with crowds, Phuket Sunday Street Market or "Phuket Walking Street" OR "Lard Yai" may suit you. It's more of a chaotic experience to witness rather than a leisurely market excursion – but the location is convenient if you're staying in Phuket town, so why not pop through for a bite to eat?

Where: Phuket Town - Thalang Road
When: Sunday 5:00pm-9pm

Chillva Night Market

Adventurous eaters, gather 'round. Chillva Night Market is serving up some appetizing and questionably appetizing local delicacies 4 days a week. You'll find salty fried bugs and worms under brightly lit tents, and you'll find freshly made ice cream being served out of mobile trucks. The coolest gimmick here, however, are the bunkbed shipping crates that have been turned into cool restaurants serving everything from Japanese to Modern Thai.

Where: Phuket Town
When: Wednesday – Saturday 5:00pm-11pm

Banzaan Fresh Market

A fresh fruit market, a clothing market and a food court all in one-Banzaan market is the perfect place to spend the afternoon out of the heat! Same fresh guava juice and sugar cane as you discover exotic fruit. Then head upstairs where you can shop for clothing, shoes, watches, and more at more reasonable prices than you'll find on the streets of Phuket! Afterwards, head to Banzaan's Thai Food Court where you can find Thai and Chinese dishes for less than 100 baht.

Where: In Patong, on Sai Kor Road, behind Jungceylon Mall
When: Daily from 7:00am – 5:00pm

Malls

There are several malls in Phuket; each one a little different than the next. Here are the top 3…

Jungceylon Mall: Located on 2nd street in Patong, Jungceylon Mall transports you back home the moment you step inside. They're got every food chain from back home: Starbucks, Burger King, Baskin Robbins, and more. There is also plenty of shopping to be done – including a NYX Makeup store!

Central Festival: Zara, H&M, The Body Shop – it's all here in Phuket Town. Central Festival is the biggest mall chain in all of Thailand, popular with both foreigners (that's us) and Thais.

Want me to plan your trip for you?
Hotels, flights, and itinerary – I got you, girl.
Message me for trip planning packages at
Alexa@TheSoloGirlsTravelGuide.com

Phuket Nightlife

Bodega Pub Crawl

It's a city tour…with booze. You'll start out at Bodega Hostel where everyone is given a Bodega Pub Crawl tank top. Throw it on and you're now all in this together. After a couple pre-party drinking games, a free bucket and shots at the hostel, the whole crew moves out to take over the city. You'll visit three of the best bars in Phuket with free shots at each bar. Weird antics, photo shoots, and cute boys from all over the world, single ladies…this one's for you.

Ps. You **don't** have to stay at Bodega in order to join the Pub Crawl! Just show up to Bodega Hostel or Bodega Resort around 9pm to sign up.

How Much: $13 USD / 450 baht
Where: Bodega Hostel Phuket
When: Monday, Wednesday, Friday at 10pm

KUDO Beach Club & Paradise Beach Club

Where daytime tanning and cocktails bleeds into sunset cocktails and flirting on the beach. Kudo Beach Club and Paradise Beach Club are the two sexiest beach clubs in Phuket. At paradise there is an entrance fee of 200 baht but get one of the best beaches in Phuket. At KUDO, there's no entry fee but you're still on Paton Beach. Plan to spend at least 1500 baht ($45 USD) per person at either of these places (there's a minimum depending on where you sit) – but with that comes prime beachfront real estate, lounge chairs, beach towels, fabulous service, all the cocktails, and usually – live DJs and a beachside or pool party.

Bangla Road

It's amazing how one stretch of road, no more than 2 blocks long, can hold so much madness. You've got Russian Strip clubs for the bachelor parties, Thai "Go-Go Bars" for every day debauchery, hole-in-the-wall people watching bars, and a few dance clubs.

Stretching from the beach, all the way back near Jungceylon Mall, it's hard to miss Bangla Road on any given night – just follow the music. This street isn't dangerous – it's just a little icky if you're sober.

There's clear prostitution and lots of fat old guys with younger Thai girls...but there's also Russian families with their children out for a bite to eat. Bangla Road is Phuket in a nutshell.

The most popular bars are Rock City, Red Hot, Sunset Bar, Shipwreck, and U2 Bar. **For dancing and nightclubs,** Illusion and White Room offer all night dance vibes that leave you sweaty and broke.

How to Get Around Phuket

Motorbikes
I do not recommend renting a motorbike in Phuket. The #1 way that tourists die in Thailand, specifically, is on a motorbike in Phuket. The roads are extremely steep, and the traffic can be intense. I don't even recommend getting on the back of a local's motorbike.

Songthaew
When you see one of these red trucks driving down the road, just wave your arm, run up to their driver-side window to tell them your destination and hop in the back. The rates range from 40-100 baht depending on where you're going. However, you can always try to haggle...especially if you've been practicing your numbers in Thai.

Tuk Tuk
Tuk Tuks are everywhere, yes. But is haggling a thing? Not really. It's standard to pay 100 or 200 baht to go anywhere. It doesn't matter if its 10-mintues down the road or two. Try haggling if you'd like – but usually the driver sets the price and doesn't budge.

Taxi
Fixed rate taxis are everywhere – schlepping their ridiculously high prices. Stick to what you're willing to pay and don't be afraid to walk away. These men will eventually give in. You can download Grab Taxi and check the estimated prices – and use that to give you an idea of what you should pay. You can try to order a Grab Taxi, but whether or not one will show up depends on the climate of the Taxi Mafia during the time of your visit. #TaxiPolitics

How to Get to Phuket?

Option 1: Fly

The only reason I wrote this big-ass Phuket chapter was because so many girls told me how convenient it was to fly from their hometown into Phuket.

If you're flying into Bangkok first, Phuket might be an easy stop over for you between islands.

➤ **By Plane via Bangkok**
Point of Departure: BKK/SVB or DMK
Duration: 1 hour & 25 minutes
Cost: Starting at $75 USD / $2,500 baht

Option 2: Take a Bus from Bangkok

➤ **By Bus**
Point of Departure: Bangkok's Southern Bus Terminal & Khao San Road
Duration: 14 hours
Cost: Starting at $21 USD / 700 baht

Fun Thai Fact
The drinking age in Thailand is 20 years old.

Getting from the Airport into Town

From Krabi International Airport

Phuket Airport is small for an international airport. It's a quick immigration and baggage claim process before you are out the doors and into Thailand.

The airport is 25 miles from Patong and takes anywhere from 45 minutes to an hour to reach your hotel – depending on how you travel.

Option 1: Fixed Rate Taxi

There are no metered taxis at Phuket Airport- only fixed rate. Prices can vary but the below prices are a good reference.

Where: You will find taxi booths inside the Arrivals Hall
How Much: (give or take 100 baht)
- ❖ Phuket Town – 400 baht
- ❖ Patong – 550 baht
- ❖ Karon – 600 baht
- ❖ Kata – 600 baht

Where: Go out of the arrival doors (you'll still be inside the airport) and you'll see a bright yellow sign with "Taxi Minibus Service" to your left and a less-obnoxiously colored but equally same-service kiosk to your right. There will also be two smaller kiosks outside of the arrival hall – again, offering the same service for the same price.

These stands also offer the Mini Bus option below.

Option 2: Mini Bus

How Much:
- ❖ Phuket Town – 150 baht
- ❖ Patong - 180 baht
- ❖ Karon – 200 baht
- ❖ Kata – 200 baht

When: The Shuttle Bus leaves when they're collected a decent number of passengers. Expect to wait up to 20 minutes for the van to fill up and leave.

Pro Tip

If the minibus stops at a tourist shop and asks you to get out…they're about to try and sell you some tours. You don't have to get out. Just stay put. Once they know that *you know*…they leave you alone. Nothing is forced or scary, just annoying.

Option 3: Pre-Booked Private Transfers

I totally recommend this option

For 100-200 baht extra, you can book a private transfer ahead of time and have a car or minivan waiting to take you to your hotel. The driver will be waiting outside arrivals holding a little sign with your name on it.

You can either arrange this with your hotel or go online and find a transfer company like PhuketShuttle.com and PhuketTransfers.com

The price depends on the car you need, but you can expect prices to be similar to these…

How Much:
- ❖   Phuket Town – 700 baht
- ❖   Patong – 680 baht
- ❖   Karon – 750 baht
- ❖   Kata – 800 baht
- ❖   Chalong Pier- 830

Fun Thai Fact
It's relatively easy to get a Student Visa for Thailand. You can stay for 1 year while you study Thai and take Thai Language Classes.

Going straight to Krabi from Phuket Airport?

You can either...

1. Arrange a Taxi from Phuket Airport to Krabi
How Long: 2 hours
How Much: $80-$100 USD

The driver picks you up at the airport and drops you directly at your hotel – any time of day or night.

2. Transfer to the pier and take a ferry
How Long: 5 hours total with the ferry, transfer and wait time
How Much: $30 USD / 1000 baht – depending on the company

Head to a taxi kiosk and get a ride to Rassada Pier.

3. Take a Public Bus
How Long: 4.5 hours
How Much: $4.50 USD / 150 baht

Hire a taxi to take you to Phuket Bus Station where you can catch the Krabi Public Bus. The bus leaves every hour. Just know that when you arrive in Krabi, you'll be dropped off at the Krabi Town Bus Station – 7.5 miles away from the beach.

The public bus is fine if you've packed light and have a Thai Sim Card or International Data. You'll need to do some navigating from the Krabi Bus Station to your hotel. OR just download "Krabi Google Maps Offline" and you can show your hotel location to a tuk tuk driver when you arrive.

Where to After Phuket?

Get out while you still have your dignity!

As always, **use the website 12Go.Asia to search for your options.** Below, I'll give you a few options so that you get an idea of what you're working with.

 Krabi, Khao Sok, Koh Lanta?

Private Taxi

Yes, Phuket is an island, but it's so close to the mainland that driving is just as convenient as taking a ferry.

To Krabi: 3 hours - $70 USD / 2300 baht
To Khao Sok: 3.3 hours- $90 USD/ 3000 baht
To Koh Lanta: 5 hours - $150USD / 4930 baht

Pro Tip

If you stumble across a private driver during your trip to Phuket, grab his business card. You can later haggle a price with him that is lower than what is listed about.

 Krabi, Koh Phi Phi, Koh Lanta, Koh Lipe, Koh Yao?

Ferry Service

From Phuket, there are multiple ferries leaving all throughout the day to nearby islands and beaches. Use the website 12Go.Asia to buy your ticket or you can arrange your ferry from a local tour office.

Here are a couple timetables from popular ferry services to give you an idea of how often your boat departs and how long your journey will be.

*Check out the back of the book for one of the ferry schedules.

 *Surat Thani, Koh Samui, Koh Tao, Koh Phangan, Krabi?*

Minivan

It's so easy to catch a bus or a minivan in Thailand – and it's cheap! For Koh Samui, Koh Phangan or Koh Tao – you'll take a bus to Surat Thani Town and from there, you'll take a ferry to the island. It's nice to buy a bundle ticket because then you don't have to worry about calculating arrival times or departure time.

Book via 12Go.Asia or buy from a tour office in Phuket. You might even want to compare prices and see which is the better deal.

> **Koh Samui, Koh Phangan**

How much: $18 - $30 USD
How Long: 7-10 hours total

- **Koh Tao**

How Much: $25-$35 USD
How Long: 10 hours ish

- **Krabi**

How Much: $25-$35 USD
How Long: 3 hours

 Koh Samui or Surat Thani?

Fly

Going to the East Coast islands like Koh Samui, Koh Phangan or Koh Tao? You can fly, but you'll need to connect in Bangkok.

> **Koh Samui**

How much: $100+ USD
How Long: 4 hours

- **Surat Thani (then take a ferry from there)**

How Much: $50+ USD
How Long: 4+ hours
Plus – ferry travel

Flying anywhere else (besides Bangkok) just doesn't make sense in this case.

Chapter 2: Koh Phi Phi

Southeast of Phuket is Koh Phi Phi, an island known for 2 things:
pristine beaches and wild parties.
You get the best of both worlds here. Spend the day snorkeling with
schools of colorful fish and the nights with booze on the beach.

This bucket-list worthy spot in Southern Thailand became popular
after the release of the movie The Beach in 2000. Since then,
travelers have been visiting Koh Phi Phi to admire the towering rock
formations, hidden beaches, fine white sand, and emerald-green
waters. A total walking island, the cobblestone streets are lined with
both western and Thai restaurants alongside clothing stalls, party
bars, and tattoo shops.

There is more to this island than meets the eye, however. Throughout
this chapter, you'll find the keys to getting tourist trail on Koh Phi
Phi…

Area Breakdown

The Phi Phi Islands are shaped like a pair of lungs. So, for this guide, we're going to break the island down into two parts: left lung and right lung.

The Right Lung

The right lung is the larger lung, abundant with stunning white sand beaches, rolling hills, and beautiful scenery. Over here, you'll find more than 100 resorts ranging from luxury hotels to budget accommodations – and plenty of adventure.

Ton Sai Bay

The heart of the Phi Phi Islands is Tonsai Bay. Lined with cobblestone streets, everything is within walking distance – including the busiest party beach, all the best restaurants, tour shops, pharmacies and anything else you'd expect to find in a small Thai tourist town.

Loh Dalum

The #1 party beach is accessible from Tonsai Bay. Here at Loh Dalum, expect a tropical exotic paradise perfect for sunbathing during the day, and wild parties with fire spinners and bucket drinks at night.

Hat Yao or Long Beach

Long Beach is known for its gorgeous hikes and viewpoints above ground, and its thriving coral reefs below. There are a handful of guest houses here, perfect if you want to get away from the social scene and into nature.

Loh Bagao Bay

As close as you'll get to a secret beach on Koh Phi Phi!

People who complain that Koh Phi Phi is too crowded have definitely not yet discovered the virgin sands of Loh Bagao Bay. Hidden on the northeast coast of Koh Phi Phi, Loh Bagao Bay is home to The Phi Phi Island Village Resort – one of the most exclusive resorts on the island. There are no tour boats, just white sand beaches and palm trees. For even more adventure, beside the resort is a small village with mangrove forest, exciting trails, bars, and restaurants.

The easiest way to get here is from Lana Bay and Nui Beach. For serious adventurers who prefer to see beautiful hills and breathtaking sceneries, try the 2-hour hike from Loh Dalum that would take about two hours. You can always hire a local guide to help you navigate the area.

Hat Laem Thong Beach

Imagine the soothing sound of the waves or the feel of fine white sand in between your toes! A kilometer-long white sand beach awaits you at Hat Laem Thong! Also called Golden Bay, Hat Laem Thong is the ideal beach for travelers who long for a quiet and relaxing holiday. This is a secluded and serene spot perfect for zenning out.

Monkey Beach

One of the best snorkeling spots on Phi Phi can be found at Monkey Beach, aka Yong Gasem Bay. More than one hundred-meters of fine white sand fill up with curious monkeys! Just watch your bag!

The Left Lung

- -

Uninhabited and unspoiled, the left lung is called "Phi Phi Leh". To preserve the eco-system, no one is allowed to stay here overnight. That means no hotels and no resorts. However, you can explore the left lung with a boat trip! Phi Phi Leh is abundant with natural cliffs, caves, and canyons waiting for you to explore!

Maya Bay

The famous "secret beach" from Leonardo DiCaprio's movie "The Beach" has recently been closed – indefinitely – in attempts to revive the damaged coral reef. Disappointing, but there is plenty more for you to see nearby.

Loh Samah Bay

Just a few minutes from Maya Bay is a small green island called Loh Samay Bay. It's the perfect snorkeling spot teeming with marine life and colorful fish.

Piley Bay

The rock formations and the turquoise waters of Piley Bay are mesmerizing. Another fantastic spot for snorkeling, the water here is crystal clear – almost magnetizing the coral below you. Here, the fish are not scared of you, surrounding your as you swim.

Accommodation in Koh Phi Phi

I'm going to give it to you straight. Here's the deal with Koh Phi Phi Accommodation…

Every hotel and hostel offer a slice of paradise…but on a party island. Don't expect super tranquil evenings with the sound of trickling water to lull you to sleep. Phi Phi is for boat trips during the day and cocktails at night. Once you accept these party vibes, you can truly enjoy your hotels for being a place to rest your head in-between some epic adventures!

Freedom Hostels@PhiPhi $

Guaranteed to give you a great night's sleep, Freedom Hostel is known for its super comfy beds, pitch black rooms, and all the air conditioning you can imagine. This is a newly renovated hostel with a lush garden on site and an inviting lobby area to meet other travelers. The shared bathrooms leave much to be desired, but for an island hostel- that's to be expected, my queen! What their bathrooms lack, their central location totally makes up for- just a short wander away from the center.

Style: Dorms
Starts at: $9 USD/ 300 baht
Where: 10 Minutes from Tonsai Pier
Address: 256 M7 T. Aonang

Blanco Beach Bar $

100% guaranteed to meet people, make friends, and have a great time when you stay at this party hostel right on the beach! Join the crazy Blanco Boat Party's to Maya Bay every day and return for beach parties and events every night. Bring your bathing suit, party

dresses… and maybe some ear plugs if you plan to go to bed early. This place is so much fun!

Style: Dorms
Starts at: $12 USD/ 160 baht
Where: 10 Minutes from Tonsai Pier - Loh Dalam Bay
Address: Loh Dalam Bay, Mu 7, Ao Nang

Uphill Cottage $

Get your cardio on, girl! The hike to Uphill Cottage will burn your glutes…but only for 5 minutes or so. Up here, you get gorgeous views of the island and something very rare on Phi Phi… total peace and quiet! Rooms are breezy with natural lighting. And every cottage has a sunny balcony where you can melt into your island vacation. Just be sure to keep an eye on the bikini you've laid out to dry…there are lots of curious monkeys up here.

Style: Privates
Starts at: $24 USD/ 800 baht
Where: Ton Sai Bay – 5-minute walk to the center
Address: Moo 7, Aonang

Viking Nature Resort $

Because a king-size bed isn't always enough, the good folks at Viking Nature resort also decided to give guests their own private hammocks on each balcony. The view from the hammock is even better.
Located on a beautiful private beach, and within walking distance to two more off-the-beaten path beaches, this is the perfect place for some alone time.

Style: Privates
Starts at: $52/1709 baht

Where: 5-minute walk to Long Beach
Address: 222 Moo.7, Aonang, Kho Phi Phi

U Rip Resort $$

Breakfast overlooking the ocean, anyone? Step straight off the restaurant steps into the sand at U Rip Resort. A brand-new resort in Phi Phi, U Rip offers comfortable hotel amenities to transport you into vacation mode on arrival. You've got a spacious pool with lounge beds, lush green jungle trees all around, a restaurant on site, gorgeous views of the island, and a tour desk to help you arrange a day of island hopping. Nestled into the hills and just a 10-minute walk to the center – you get the best of both worlds at U Rip.

Style: Privates
Starts at: $50 USD/ 1665 baht
Where: Tonsai Bay
Address: 65 moo.7 T. Ao-nang

The Cobble Beach $$

Pick your poison. There's an infinity pool overlooking the sea and the beautiful beach with warm ocean water only a 2-minute walk from your bed. If you plan on being in your bikini all day, The Cobble Beach offers you the perfect opportunity. Breakfast is included, and staff will help you book any tour you want. Everything you need is right here.

Style: Privates
Starts at: $73 USD/ 2330 baht
Where: Main Beach
Address: 9/12 Moo 7, Phi Phi Island

Phi Phi Relax Beach Resort $$

Located right on the water, the Phi Phi Relax Beach Resort doesn't overcomplicate its natural beauty with enhancements. Instead, it features the stunning natural beauty as a part of the experience, offering snorkeling adventures and kayaks to its guests, welcoming you to take in all there is to see and do on the popular island. Traditional fisherman boats take guests out on the water to explore neighboring islands for a day adventure, before returning for a freshly prepared meal in the on-site restaurant. It's luxury living with a rustic twist, perfect for a short stay or long holiday.

Style: Privates
Starts at: $79 USD/ 2,614 baht

Where: 1 mile from Loh Lana Bay
Address: Phaknam Bay, Phi Phi Island Ao Nang

P.P. Blue Sky Resort $$$

Location, location, location. P.P. Blue Sky Resort is tucked into the trees on long beach, just steps from the sand. Eat breakfast by the beach with an undisturbed view of the waves crashing on the shore. P.P. Blue Sky Resort is the peaceful getaway that you needed. Take some 'me time' in your private bungalow or grab a snorkel and get in touch with your inner mermaid.

Style: Privates
Starts at: $90 USD/ 3000 baht
Where: Long Beach
Address: Longbeach, Koh Phi Phi, 138/2, Moo 7

PP Charlie Beach Resort $$$

Party girls...you're going to want to check out PP Charlie Beach Resort. Nicer than a hostel but not as button-up as a resort - here is your happy medium where you can finally meet travelers outside of the budget backpacker scene. Daily pool parties with live DJs offer the perfect opportunity to mingle with cute boys and fellow travel girls.

Heads up: if you're looking for peace a quiet – it's only found after the clubs die down! Sleep when you're dead, babe.

Style: Privates

Starts at: $115 USD/ 3777 baht
Where: Central
Address: 104 Moo 7, PP Island

Phi Phi Island Village Beach Resort $$$$

Here's that secret beach I was talking about – Loh Bagao Bay! While this virgin white sand beach with warm turquoise water isn't officially private, it's hidden...unless you're staying at Phi Phi Island Village Beach Resort, that is.

Tucked away from the hustle and bustle that Phi Phi is known for, you'll forget that you're in a backpacker's paradise. This resort is welcoming, exotic and luxurious with tropical trees, bungalows and décor that instantly transports you into vacation mode. Service is top-notch, perhaps the best on the island with English-speaking staff, room service, and massages whenever you wish.

Fair warning: Your Instagram followers may double once you start posting pictures of your exotic island vacay in Loh Bagao Bay.

Style: Privates
Starts at: $360 USD/ 11,912 baht
Where: Loh Lana Bay
Address: 49 Moo 8, Phi Phi Island, Ao Nang

Where to Eat on Koh Phi Phi

Everything is within walking distance on Koh Phi Phi. Just start wandering around and you'll get familiar with the cobble stone streets and establishments in no time.

Only Noodles Pad Thai

This island restaurant makes one dish and one dish only- and damn, do they make it well. Choose your style of noodles and your protein and you'll have fresh Pad Thai made to order for less than 100 baht.

Dubliners Irish Pub

Burgers, Bangers, and Banana Pancakes- when you need flavor from home, Dubliner's has got you covered. You can expect tasty western food at western prices that come in massive portions to hit the spot.

Tuk's BBQ

Head over to Reggae Bar and keep your eye out for the street vendor grilling up smokey sticks of meat and veggies starting at 30 baht each. This is true to the Thai Street Food tradition that every traveler should experience.

Papaya

Eat where the locals eat…and where the tourists eat! Everyone eats at Papaya and for good reason- their Thai food and Indian dishes are incredible! Made with Muslim influence, you've got your choice of classic garlic prawns or get eastern with some freshly made naan and curry. As this place is a Muslim establishment, BYOB.

….oh, and **McDonalds.** Yep. That's here now.

Highlights & Activities

Go Scuba Diving
You can either party or Scuba – but you can't do both.

If you want to get your Open Water Dive Certificate, Koh Phi Phi is a pretty gorgeous place to do so. But you must commit to 4 days of PADI Dive Classes with no boozing it up at night.

Get to bed early and you'll be rewarded with some of the most beautiful dive sites in the world. There are ship wrecks to see, manta rays to swim with and even small sharks to help you cross a big ticket off your bucket list. The course usually lasts 3-4 days and often, comes with a discount on accommodation so pick your dive center first, and hotel second.

Ps. Plan a week in Phi Phi and you **can** party after the course.

How Much: Open Water courses typically start at $103 USD / 3,500 bah

Koh Phi Phi Viewpoint
If you swipe through Tinder in Thailand, you'll come across the same scenic photo where a dude is standing on top of a mountain and below is a narrow strip of land between two beaches. That's this place. The hike offers 3 viewpoints that reach up to 186 m above sea level. The walk is only about 15-25 minutes but get ready to sweat-it's steep!

How Much: $1 USD/ 30 baht (for the first 2 viewpoints) and $1.75 USD /50 baht (for the 3rd)

Monkey Beach
Most island-hopping tours on offer make a stop at Monkey Beach, a gorgeous stretch of sand inhabited by the curios macaques. There's tons of them ready to take selfies with you…but they are also ready to take your shit. If it is not securely attached to your body, these little thieves will run with it – hats, water bottles, even earrings are a risky move. The monkeys however are mostly harmless, but they do have an ego, so don't tease them.

So, while you can visit Monkey Beach with a tour – the beach is more enjoyable before the crowds get there. I suggest venturing over to Monkey Beach on foot, with a kayak or if you're hiring a longtail boat for a private tour, go to Monkey Beach first.

Ibiza Pool Party

The biggest pool party on Koh Phi Phi! Pack a cute suit - you're not going to want to miss this! Every Tuesday, Thursday and Sunday from 1pm – 9pm, Ibiza throws a giant pool party where travelers gather to drink, swim and socialize alongside live DJ spinning some island-worthy tunes. With drink specials, beer pong, and a diverse mix of international travelers – Ibiza Pool Party kind of feels like a pool party that you'd find in Vegas…. but way cheaper and no entry fee. This is the perfect opportunity for you solo girls to make some friends- the vibes here are always super welcoming.

How Much: $8 USD / 200 baht admission that includes one free drink

The Best Tours

Phi Phi Pirate Boat Booze Cruise

What would a pirate boat be without drunken sailors? While most boat tours frown upon drinking alcohol on board, the Phi Phi Pirate Boat brings the liquor for you! You'll spend the day partying AND sightseeing along with a DJ, insane views, and amazing captains to lead the adventure.

The tour stops at the most popular destinations, including Monkey Beach, Viking Cave, Pilleh Lagoon, Loh Samah Bay and Sunset Point. You'll have the option of snorkeling, kayaking, or just relaxing on board with a beer. Take off is at 12:30 every afternoon with the tour ending at sunset. All you need is a swim suit and a ticket, and one of those is optional.

Pro Tip

If you've come to Phi Phi alone and want to make friends fast – this is the way to do it.

Starts at: $39/ 1300
Where: Phi Phi Pier

Rock Climbing

Phi Phi only get more beautiful the higher up you go. The bad boy to climb on this island is Tonsai Tower, a 450-foot natural rock wall with up nearly 30 moderate routes. Push yourself and you'll be rewarding with stunning views of the island and crystal blue water. Want more? Ibex Rock Climbing also offers destination climbs where you hop in a boat in search of more natural courses.

During a half-day or full day excursion, you'll learn the basics of rock climbing in a fun and safe environment with certified staff who tailor every lesson to your abilities and goals. All necessary equipment is provided for you and climbing session last 4-8 hours, either in the morning or afternoon – it's up to you.

Starts at: $23/ 750 baht
Contact: Ibex Rock Climbing

Island Hopping

You'll see full-day and half-day tours being offered everywhere you look on Koh Phi Phi. On these tours, you'll pile into a longtail boat or a speed boat with other travelers and visit the most popular beaches and islands in the area. There will be lots of swimming, snorkeling and photo opps during your island-hopping tour.

The most popular spots to look forward to:
- Monkey Beach with all the moneys!
- Pileh Lagoon
- Loh Samah Bay

Heads Up: The famous secret beach from Leonardo DiCaprio's "The Beach" aka Maya Bay, is no longer available for tours. They've closed this bay indefinitely due to the deterioration of coral... which, good for them for taking care of the environment.

How Much: Starting at $30 USD / 1,000 baht

Markets & Shopping

There are family-owned local shops in Phi Phi Islands that are open until 9 pm or 11 pm. Gift shops open until 10 pm. Although there are no hospitals in the island, they do have a local health center located in Tonsai Bay. Two bakeries serve the best cakes and other delectable goods.

Tonsai Waking Streets
Tonsai is shopping heaven. The streets are lined with boutiques, tattoo shops, cheap Thai tank top shops and everywhere you look you'll find something fluorescent!

A couple recommendations: There's **Phi Phi Market** with a selection of typical Thai tourist stalls which sell tank tops and trinkets. **Namily** is a French owned boutique selling bags and dresses on central Tonsai and **Mr. Rum Boutique** sells the clothing ideal for island living with flowy dresses and colorful tops – located on Tonsai main street

Fun Thai Fact
Thailand used to be named "Siam." On May 11th, 1949, Siam was officially renamed as the Kingdom of Thailand.

Koh Phi Phi Nightlife

So, listen. Koh Phi Phi is one of the best party islands in Southeast Asia. In fact, partying is the main activity for travelers who stay on Koh Phi Phi. Don't fight it.

Banana Bar

Photo Credit: Banana Bar

Beer pong, flip cup, movie nights, live streaming of sport matches and all around fun vibes- Banana Bar is possibly the most famous party spot on Phi Phi. Not to mention, they've got some of the best western food to help you soak up that alcohol.

Where: Central Tonsai– you'll walk past it everyday

Phi Phi Reggae Bar

Muay Thai and Mojitos are the perfect combination for a rowdy night on this island paradise. Fights kick off at 9pm for an organized slice of chaos. Lots of opportunity to mingle with strangers and have a fun time. In the same vicinity of Jordan's Irish Pub in Tonsai Village, it's inevitable that you'll eventually gravitate here.

The Main Beach / Loh Dalum Beach

Follow the flock and wander down to the main beach lined with a collection of bars whose patrons melt together to create one big party. Some bars paint everyone with florescent face paint, others have bean bags on the beach positioned to watch the fire show, and most offer massive fishbowl buckets of booze to get tipsy.

The most popular bars you'll find are **Slinky Bar** where they light rope on fire and drunk people try to jump rope (fun to watch but a stupid idea), **Ibiza** with the pool parties mentioned earlier, and **Carlito's** which stays open officially until 2am.

Pro Tip

Skip the buckets. The booze they use might be homemade and give you a terrible hangover. Beer is a safer bet.

Classy Girl Tip

OR just buy your own bottle of Whiskey from 7-Eleven, keep it in your purse, order soda and mix it under the table. You think I'm kidding? I'm not.

Sunflower Beach Bar

Also, on Loh Dalum Beach, Sunflower Deserves its own mention.

Using remnants of the 2004 Tsunami, "Captain" – a tsunami survivor – has created a memorial and bar in honor of the friends and family that he has lost. Instead of a somber spot, Sunflower Beach Bar is a place where life is celebrated. It's a place to mingle and meet travelers from all over the world and enjoy life together! Once the sun goes down, there are fire shows and acoustic guitar performances to ease you into those island vibes. No shoes needed.

Where: On the viewpoint end of Loh Dalum Beach

Hippies Bar

Devastated in the 2004 Tsunami, Hippies Bar is back and better than ever. Take your shoes off and stick your toes in the sand while you set up shop at a driftwood table under the palm trees, overlooking the ocean. Hippies Bar streams live sports events from home and also plays live music after 8pm along with fire dancing and DJs. Cocktails are decently priced, and food is fantastic.

Where: Tonsai East - Beachfront by Phi Phi Villa Resort

Full Moon Party

For adventure-seekers and partygoers visiting Thailand, it's almost a sin not to attend one of the monthly Full Moon Parties – at least once in your life! So epic, that backpackers and travellers from all over the world flock to Thailand just to experience this wild event.

While the Full Moon Part is most famously help on Koh Phangan – Koh Phi Phi also throws a pretty epic Full Moon Party, too. It's slightly smaller than Koh Phangan's Full Moon Party but less overwhelming if you're not a hardcore party girl.

How do you buy tickets? You don't need to pre-buy tickets, just show up and pay 100 baht – which partially goes towards a beach clean- up post-event. Once you're in, you buy drinks like normal – bucket drinks are usually $10 / 300 baht.

Where is it? On Koh Phi Phi, the Full Moon Party is help on the main beach aka Loh Dalum Beach.

How to Get Around Koh Phi Phi

Walk

Phi Phi is a walking island with paved roads and trodden dirt paths.
No need to rent a bike or a tuk tuk.
That was easy.

How to Get to Koh Phi Phi

By Boat

No airports or bridges here – you've got to hop in a speedboat to get your cute butt here.

 From Phuket

Head to Rassada Pier

How Much: $22 - $30 USD / 723 – 1000 baht
How Long: 1 – 2 hours

PHUKET - PHI PHI Ferry Schedule		PHI PHI - PHUKET Ferry Schedule	
DEPARTURE	ARRIVAL	DEPARTURE	ARRIVAL
Phuket: 08:30	Phi Phi: 10:30	Phi Phi: 09:00	Phuket: 11:00
Phuket: 11:00	Phi Phi: 12:30	Phi Phi: 14:00	Phuket: 15:40
Phuket: 13:30	Phi Phi: 15:30	Phi Phi: 14:30	Phuket: 16:30
Phuket: 15:00	Phi Phi: 16:30		

 From Koh Lanta

Head to Koh Lanta Saladan Pier

How Much: $14 - $20 USD / 460 - 600 baht
How Long: 30 minutes – 1.5 hours
When: 8:00am, 9am, 11:30am and 1:30pm

 **From Krabi**

How Much: $15 USD / 500 baht
How Long: 1 – 1.45 hours

KRABI - PHI PHI Ferry Schedule	
DEPARTURE	ARRIVAL
Krabi: 09:00	Phi Phi: 10:30
Krabi: 10:30	Phi Phi: 12:15
Krabi: 13:30	Phi Phi: 15:00
Krabi: 15:00	Phi Phi: 16:45
Krabi: 16:00	Phi Phi: 17:45

PHI PHI - KRABI Ferry Schedule	
DEPARTURE	ARRIVAL
Phi Phi: 09:00	Krabi: 10:45
Phi Phi: 10:30	Krabi: 12:00
Phi Phi: 13:30	Krabi: 15:15
Phi Phi: 15:30	Krabi: 17:00

Ps. When you get off the pier, you'll be asked to pay a 20 baht Environment Fee.

Chapter 3: Krabi & Railay

Heaven on earth! Just a quick 1-hour flight from Bangkok and a 3-hour drive from Phuket, Krabi is the ultimate Thailand vacation destination with crystal blue water, white sand beaches, and coconut cocktails.

@aforeigner.abroad

Once you're here, you can plan on any budget or throw cash around like Oprah. Live it up in fancy resorts or party barefoot with local expats – you've got all the options! Most attractive about Krabi, however, are the skyscraper islands that tower over warm blue water and powdery-soft sand beaches like a scene out of Avatar. Plan to live in your bathing suit with beach days and boat tours!

Area Breakdown

Krabi Town

A main hub for transportation and commerce, Krabi Town offers a peek into local life with cheap street food and bustling restaurants filled with Thai people. Take your pick of affordable guest houses near to the bus station or along the river. Your money goes far in this neck of the woods. To get to the beach from here, you'll need to take some form of transportation – Songthaews are a good option, walking is not.

Ao Nang Beach

The main tourist area, Ao Nang Beach is highlighted by one very long road in an 'L-Shape' that stretches up down the hill from town and then curves along the beach. The entirety of this massive road is lined with hostels, bars, restaurants, tourist desks and of course, tons of shopping where you can buy swim suits, sun glasses, snorkel gear and more.

Nopparat Thara Beach

Just over one mile west of Ao Nang Beach is Nopparat Thara Beach, which is part of Nopparat Thara Beach & Mu Ko Phi Phi National Park. While this beach is not a swimming beach, it is an exploring beach!

The first half of the beach is not too impressive, with grainy sand and mushy shore – but keep going! The very west-end of NT Beach is stunning. There's white powder sand, beachy bridges with shallow water on each side, a few islands to explore and tons of shady spots for a picnic.

The road that lines the beach has plenty of shops, restaurants, and massage parlors, making this a great daytime adventure. Pop into Talay Bar for a couple drinks and a snack.

Railay

There is a peninsula jetting off from Ao Nang Beach that is absolutely stunning and not to be missed! You'll find four beaches here.

- **Railay West-** This is the main beach where most long tail boats dock – letting you off into sandy paradise. Swim, tan & play here.

- **Tonsai Beach-** When the tide is low, you can climb through the rocks where you'll find a large resort on the sand and a hippie paradise back into the jungle.

- **Phra Nang Cave Beach** – Secluded and insanely beautiful, this is the beach you came to Thailand to see! You can easily walk to here via the concrete path on Railay East. Bring some snacks and drinks and spend the afternoon here.

- **Railay East** – Where the party happens! Railay East is not really a beach, more of a cove with high and low tides, highlighted by a concrete path that is lined with hotels, restaurants and bars. In the center of the path is the boat pier, Phra Nang Cave Beach is to the very right and party central with restaurants and bars is to the left.

Accommodation in Krabi Province

Krabi Province is quite big and includes Krabi Town, Ao Nang Beach, Railay Beach, and Tonsai. Got all that? Let's break it down…

Krabi Town Accommodation

Closer to the airport than the beach, Krabi Town offers a taste of authentic Thai culture with riverside hotels, night markets, temples, and motorbike adventures.

Staying in Krabi Town is a fun way to spend your last (or first) day or two.

Slumber Party Krabi Town $

Wanna get weird? Here's where you come to do that. Slumber Party never sleeps. You'll meet tons of travelers from all over the world. Together you will go on Pub Crawls, play drinking games, go on beach excursions and boat tours… then bond over how bad your hangover is the morning after. This hostel is located at the very top of the road that leads down to the beach – you can't walk to the beach, but Slumber Party will take care of that with free beach transfers 4x per day. This is a good option for when their beach location is full – which happens often.

Style: Dorms
Starts at: $11 USD/ 370 baht
Address: 376/41 Ao Nang

Snoozz Hotel $

If you've got an early flight, it's always a good idea to stay in town the night before. Get some shut eye at Snoozz Hotel, a quiet place with all-girl dorm rooms. They offer airport transfers for a small charge, have helpful English-speaking staff and a yummy café in the lobby where you can grab a quick bite before you travel.

Style: Dorms and Privates
Starts at: $7.50 USD /250 baht
Address: 52 Maharaj 6 Road, Muang District

Just Fine Krabi $

Not a backpacker's hostel, but not a fancy hotel either – Just Fine Krabi is just fine for the solo traveling girl who wants clean sheets and a central location. Your stay, however, will be more than "just fine" in this nautical themed hotel that is as charming as it is comfortable. The rooms are spacious, there is a social living room to meet other travelers, and the prime location next to the night market and cafes means that you can explore on foot, all without over-spending!

Style: Privates
Starts at: $25 USD / 800 baht
Address: 2/8 Maharach 10, T.Paknam

Family Tree Hotel $$

After a week of living in your bathing suit, sometimes you just want to clean up, wash your hair, and watch the news. Family Tree Hotel is the perfect place to do that before you head to the airport the next day. You can even add a last dose of adventure into your itinerary as this hotel is within walking distance to the night market and a short ride away from Tiger Cave Temple. Alternatively, if you're using Krabi as a jumping off point to Koh Lanta or a nearby destination, this is a convenient spot for smooth transport.

Style: Privates
Starts at: $45 USD/ 1,500 baht
Address: 6 Maharaj Soi.2 Rd., Paknam, Mueang

Ao Nang Beach Accommodation

Ao Nang is the main beach on the mainland. Staying here means that you can shop to your heart's content and go on island hopping tours during the day, then hit up some restaurants and bars with live music at night.

Slumber Party by the Beach $

It'ssss party time. My #1 vote for budget backpackers, social girls, and single ladies in Krabi. Slumber Party is a super social hostel that offers adventures during the day and wild parties at night. Home to Thailand's Biggest Pub Crawl, it's impossible not to make friends here. When your hangover subsides, gather up those new friends for boat trips, kayaking adventures, and beach days with **free** breakfast, nightly cocktail shots, group BBQ & more.

Style: Dorms
Starts at: $13 USD/ 440 baht
Address: Ao Nang Beach

Stay Over Hostel $

Social, clean, and safe with a fabulous location. Stay Over Hostel ticks all the boxes and then some. If you want to be social but your liver needs a break, this is the place for you. The main attraction here is the rooftop with bright green turf with cozy pillows and resort-level views of the Krabi Cliffside. Hang out with fellow travelers for a chill night by the beach.

Style: Dorms
Starts at: $11 USD/ 370 baht
Address: Moo2, Aonang, Meung Krabi

M Boutique & Kitchen $

If you're on a budget and aren't really the "dorm room" type of girl - M Boutique & Kitchen offers a happy medium of privacy and price. Each room has its own little balcony looking down at the main road. Set off on foot about 10-15 minutes and you'll reach the beach. Come back to solitude in your simple, but pleasant room to regroup.

Style: Privates
Starts at: $20 USD/ 670 baht
Address: 43 Moo 2, Tumbol Aonang, Aumphur Meung Krabi

PhuPha Aonang Resort $$

Private bungalows and pool nestled amongst a lush tropical garden with friendly service, fabulous breakfast and free shuttles to the beach…this is exactly what you imagined when you pictured coming to Thailand. Tucked away on a side-street off the main drag, you're just a 10-minute walk from the action. Afterwards, you can come back to your little slice of paradise, listen to the crickets and watch the stars.

Style: Privates
Starts at: $38 USD/ 1,300 baht
Address: 395 Moo 2, Soi 13, Muang, Ao Nang

Phra Nang Inn by Vacation Village $$

You came here for the beach, right? Phra Nang Inn puts you 30-seconds from the sand without breaking the bank. Wake up and eat breakfast with views of palm trees and the ocean. When you're ready for an adventure, you're just steps from all the tourist kiosks offering every boat tour imaginable! After your day in the sun, come back and swim in the jungle-esque pool surrounded by lush greenery. Phra Nang Inn offers free cooking classes, handicraft workshops and dancing classes throughout the week – ask the front desk!

Heads Up: You can hear music from nearby bars til about midnight.

Pro Tip

For the best view, ask for room #2469 when you book

Style: Privates
Starts at: $55 USD/ 1,900 baht
Address: 119 Moo 2 Aonang, Muang, Krabi

Railay & Tonsai Beach Accommodation

Both Railay Beach and Tonsai Beach offer access to pristine beaches and islands, as well as rock climbing, kayaking, and a plethora of beach bars and restaurants.

To get to Tonsai, walk to the end of the main beach on Railay. When the tide is low during the day, you can climb through a rock tunnel. When the tide is high, you will have a long-tail boat zip you over.

Chill Out Bar & Bungalow $

No shoes, no bra, no problem. Chill Out Bar is an oasis away from the tourists and away from civilization where you never know what time it is…and it doesn't even matter. Forget your troubles as you take a kayak out for a spin, play a card game with strangers, or learn to rock climb cause YOLO. Minimalistic and simplistic – hit the reset button on life, babe.

Style: Dorms and Bungalows
Starts at: $7 / 200 baht
Address: Tonsai Beach

Blanco Hideout Hostel $

The first and only hostel in Railay, this place is kind of a big deal. Blanco Hideout is a brand-new hostel located on Railay East in the middle of all the action! Check in, throw your bags down, and go exploring on foot! You're 5-minutes from Phra Nang Cave Beach and right next to the best bars and restaurants. The hostel does a pub crawl three times a week (Monday, Wednesday and Friday) with a 2-hour open-bar at Blanco where you can mingle with other travelers. Plus, there's a big pool overlooking the water next to a little lounging deck with amazing views. What more do you need?

Style: Dorms and Privates
Starts at: $9 USD/ 220 baht
Location: Railay East

Tonsai Bay Resort $$

Tonsai Bay Resort is a new-ish resort that has access to the entire bay. There are private villas with balconies or cozy double rooms with all the amenities, just a stone's throw away from the beach. Staying here means enjoying nature as you're tucked into the jungle next to rock climbing and paddle boarding. At night, head inland away from the beach and into the jungle where you'll find a Peter-Pan style neverland of bars and restaurants with barefoot Thai guys and stoner expats who will all be happy to see you.

Style: Privates
Starts at: $28 USD/ 950 baht
Location: Tonsai Beach
How to Get There: Take a longtail boat directly to Tonsai Beach or walk through the rocks from Railay Beach.

Railay Princess Resort and Spa $$$

Fantastic bang for your buck over on Railay East, Princess Resort and Spa would easily cost 3x the price back home…but because it's Thailand, you get two massive pools, a spacious room with a private balcony and the best buffet breakfast in Railay starting at $40 per night. Located directly in the center of Railay East, 20-meters from the pier, you really can't go wrong staying here.

Style: Private
Starts at: $40 USD/ 1,200 baht
Address: Railay East

Railay Bay Resort $$$

Pamper yourself at Railay Bay Resort, located right on the beach! Start your morning with an amazing breakfast buffet on the water where you can watch the longtail boats putter in and out. Then, roll into the only pool on Railay that directly overlooks the ocean. You can get a private room or a secluded villa! The villas are totally private with lounge beds and a mini outdoor pool! Tan naked and fill the little pool up with shower gel for a skinny-dipping bubble bath.

Style: Privates
Starts at: $55 USD/ 1,900 baht
Address: Railay Beach

Avatar Railay $$

A 4-star resort with 2-star prices? Yes, please. Avatar is by far one of my favorite hotels in all of Thailand. The pool-access room is incredible! You get a private balcony with stairs leading into the pool and your own cabana bed. If you don't mind spending a little extra…you can get a villa with a private pool for around $120 – if you book early, that is. Step outside of the hotel and you're on the concrete path that takes you to Railay East nightlife *and* Phra Nang Cave Beach. Ugh, this place is seriously paradise.

Style: Privates
Starts at: $68 USD/ 2,300 baht
Location: East Railay Beach

Where to Eat in Krabi Province

It's impossible to run out of food options in Krabi. You'll find tons of restaurants and bars up and down the main road leading down to Ao Nang Beach. Everything from authentic Thai food to amazing Indian and everything in-between. You'll find that a lot of restaurants and bars offer similar menus and cocktail prices- but here are a couple favorites to be on the lookout for....

Krabi Town

Chao Fah Night Market
Street food is calling! For 30-60 baht per plate, you can try every Thai dish under the sun alongside southern Muslim curries and Chinese wok dishes. Set in a 1400 sqm. parking lot, there are plenty of tables and chairs mixed in with stall after stall of fresh flavors to taste- there is something here for every palate.

Open: Daily from 5pm – Midnight
Location: Chao Fah Pier – Krabi Town
How to Get There: Jump in a 20 - 40 baht Songthaew

Baitoey Restaurant
Dinner with a view, this Thai restaurant is located across the street from the river where you can watch boats coming in and out underneath the palm trees. The food here is tasty and offers some of the best shellfish and crab in Krabi Town. Paired with the Papaya Salad – you've got a fabulous meal that is light and fresh. A bit more upscale with high-quality ingredients, don't expect street food prices. This place might break the bank at $8 per plate!

Open: Daily 10am-10pm
Location: 79 Khongkha road, Pak Nam, Krabi Town
How to Get There: Walk along the river, 5 minutes south of the night market

Gecko Cabane Restaurant
A casual Thai restaurant with cheap beer and classic dishes, Gecko Cabane is a great place to pop in for lunch or a laid-back dinner. The staff are fabulously hospitable and attentive – they certainly are not on Thai time here! You can expect friendly service along with Thai dishes that represent what Thai people typically eat on any given day in the South of Thailand. Oh, and don't worry about your food being

too spicy- they staff usually ask how spicy you'd like your dish on a 1-10 scale!

Open: Daily 11am-2pm & 5pm-11pm
Location: 1/36-37 Soi Ruamjit, Maharat Road, Krabi Town
How to Get There: Walk 10 minutes west of the night market, into town along Soi Ruamjit

Ao Nang Beach

Krabi Cafe 8.98

When you want a real fresh fruit smoothie or fruit juice that isn't half sugar – this is the place to go. The perfect spot before a day of tours or hikes, give yourself a kick of vitamins and fiber with a yummy Granola Bowl or pack in the protein with a proper eggs bene to go along with your "green + clean" juice.

Open: 7am-11pm
Address: 143/7-8, Ao Nang
How to Get There: 5-minutes up Ao Nang Road on the left

The Last Fisherman Bar

Eat dinner with your toes in the sand right next to the crashing waves! The Last Fisherman Bar is a casual restaurant underneath the trees that brings in freshly-caught seafood every day! Food is extremely well-priced considering the million-dollar ocean front view. Expect dishes to be anywhere from 200 baht – 800 baht made with fresh ingredients. Cocktails start at 180 baht - a small price to pay to watch the sun set in Thailand.

Open: 10am – 11pm
Location: Ao Nang Beachfront
How to Get There: Where the main road first hits Ao Nang beach, go left down the foot path until you cross under a sign that says The Last Fisherman Bar.

Crazy Gringos

Live music. Sports on the flat screen. Easy people watching. Crazy Gringos is the epitome of a "vacation bar" filled with expats and vacationers looking for a taste of home. Famous for their chicken wings and cocktails, you could easily spend all evening at this bar without breaking the bank. With lots of solo travelers passing through, Crazy Gringo's is an easy place to start up a conversation with a stranger!

Open: 3pm-1am
Address: 459/2 4203, Tambon Ao Nang
How to Get There: Located inside the small shopping alley at the curve of the L-shaped Ao Nang Road.

Lotus Court Restaurant

Oysters, lobster tails, salmon steak, Wagyu beef burgers and nitrogen ice cream made at the table- treat yo self, girl. Lotus Court is on the upscale-side of dining but for Thai prices. Order a bottle of wine, melt into the tunes of live piano music, and leave without having spent a fortune.

Open: Daily 11:30 - Midnight
Address: 396-396/1 Moo 2 | Centara Grand Beach Resort & Villas Krabi
How to Get There: Walk to Centara Grand Beach Resort

Railay Beach

One Stop Take Away Shop

Vegans and Vegetarians will fall in love with One Stop, aka Govinda's at the Beach. When you've had a long day and you're craving some clean eating, this place has Veggie Pizza, Hummus, Soy Meat Burritos, Cheese Empanadas...you name it. They've also got a huge menu of sweet treats like Oreo milkshakes and fruit smoothies to cool you down!

Open: Breakfast-Dinner
Location: East side of Railay Beach

Railay Family Restaurant

Eating grilled shrimp and fried rice out of a pineapple underneath a straw-thatched roof hut- it doesn't get more Thailand than this! Unsurprisingly, this place gets pretty popular around dinner time and will be the only restaurant with a line- but trust me, it's worth the wait.

Open: Daily Lunch til Close

Location: Between Railay Beach and East Railay Beach
Address: 354 Moo 2, Railay Beach

Railay Rapala Rock Wood Resort

Nachos. Pizza. Indian. Vegetarian. Vegan. When you're craving something other than Thai food on Railay Beach, this is the place to go. Nestled in the jungle, Rapala is a tranquil experience with yummy food where you can eat in peace with a good book and a cold beer or Iced Coffee.

Open: 10am-10pm
Location: Railay East

Coffee Station

Remember Owl from Winnie the Pooh? As owls do, he lived comfortably in a little wooden nook where his friends gathered for tea and a chat. The same goes for Coffee Station, except in place of tea, you have freshly ground Italian Coffee prepared right before your eyes. The coffee is strong, there is a book swap station, and the Thai staff who sleeps upstairs are some of the friendliest guys you'll meet.

Open: Morning til night
Location: Railay – next to Jamaica Bar

A couple more mentions...

Friendship Restaurant – Yummy breakfast and coffee
Local- The best deep friend Papaya Salad ever!
Last Bar – Great Thai food at local prices
Joy Beach Bar – Wood fire pizza

Highlights & Activities

The Krabi Province, including Ao Nang Beach, Railay Beach and Tonsai Beach, is quite compact. Any tour that you want to go on can be reached from any of the above locations. It doesn't matter where you stay- there is a long-tail boat waiting to take you to your destination. So, let's get into it...

Tab Kak Hang Nak Hill Nature Trail

Half scooter and half feet – this is a bucket list adventure for my girls who like to get sweaty.

Tab Kak Hang Nak Hill Nature Trail is a true hike through the jungle on a moderately steep 2.5-mile path. The paths are clearly marked to keep you on track as you make your way over little bridges, under tall jungle canopy and on top of pure earth, rocks, and roots at your feet.

During the two to three-hour trek, you will come across stunning vistas and viewpoints of rolling mountains and crystal blue shores. Along the way, you'll find small natural waterfalls and swimming holes. Then at the very top, you'll reach the 360-degree viewpoint – called Hang Na Cape - that makes the whole butt-burning hike worth it.

To Get There: Drive an hour out of Krabi Town to Khao Ngon Nak National Park. At the entrance of the park, you'll find a little parking lot next to the trail entrance. At the trail entrance, there will be a big map of the trail, the paths, and the viewpoints that you want to look out for along the way.

Pro Tip

Start in the morning and check the weather! You don't want to hike in a downpour!

The Emerald Pool

The Emerald Pool is this gorgeous blue, almost glowing, natural spring in the middle of the jungle! The water is cool and crystal clear with little streams and mini pools surrounding it– perfect for swimming! To reach the Emerald Pool, you'll stroll along a jungle path leading to smaller pools and the Blue Pool (closed May-October) scattered along the way. Stop and swim wherever you please.

The trick to enjoying the Emerald Pool is to go in the morning before the crowd! Drive yourself on a motorbike or hire a tuk tuk driver to take you so that you can avoid the organized van tour times that make the Emerald Pool feel like a public pool.

Entrance Fee: 30 baht
Open: 8:00am – 5:00pm

Krabi Hot Springs

Riiiiight nearby The Emerald Pool you can find these natural hot springs that reach up to 95-107 F (35-42 C). Just like the Emerald Pool, the hot springs are surrounded by forest with hot little pools and waterfalls where you can climb, swim, and soak. There is also a cool river at the base of the hot springs where you can take a refreshing dip at the end of your natural spa day!

To get there on your own, literally just plug "Krabi Hot Springs" into the GPS and you're all set. Once you reach the parking lot, you go through a gate and pay a small entrance fee. Follow the grey brick path where you'll pass the first hot spring – but this one looks more like a sparkly swimming pool with concrete bottom.

Tiger Cave Temple

What does 1,237 steps up a Thai mountain get you? A 360 -degree panoramic view of Krabi Town along with a gorgeous Buddhist Temple that glistens in the sun! This Buddhist Temple dates back to 1975, founded by monk looking to meditate in peace….who instead found a cave full of tigers. This spot became sacred for the monks, who adorned the mountain with golden Buddhist statues and shrines. Plan to spend 1-hour hiking and 30 minutes wandering…and 5 minutes to buy some bananas and feed the monkeys.

Pro Tip

Dress respectfully by covering your shoulders and knees.

Open: All day
Location: About 2 miles from Krabi Town
To Get There: Rent a motorbike for ~$5 and follow the signs OR hire a tuk tuk driver to take you up.

Explore Phra Nang Cave Beach

Staying on Railay? You can access one of the most beautiful beaches you've ever seen via an easy, concrete-paved path. Located on the East Side of Railay, just follow the signs or ask a local to point you in the right direction. As you follow the path, you walk underneath some trees – look up! This is where the monkeys live. There is a penis-shrine temple (yes, you read that right) tucked in a cave and a steep hike/rock climb you can take (before the penises on the path, you'll see a long rope and red clay where people climb) that offers gorgeous views of the area. Bring snacks and a beach towel and hang out here all-day long.

Go Rock Climbing on Tonsai Beach

The natural cliff edge on Tonsai is a rock climbers dream. In fact, rock climbers travel near and far just to scale the cliff with gorgeous views of the sand and water below. The rock climbing crew has up-to-date gear and offers lessons for beginners and advanced climbers.

Where: Tonsai Beach
Price: Starting at $24 USD / 800 baht with Basecamp Tonsai

Ya's Thai Cookery School Class

While you'll find tons of fabulous cooking schools in Krabi – this is the cooking class that I took and loved. You'll start your day at the market shopping for fresh ingredients to whip up 6 Thai dishes. The chef, Ya, speaks English and has a great sense of humor – so don't worry about being a master chef! Just have fun.

After every course is cooked, you'll sit down to eat! When the class is over, you'll go home with a recipe book and perhaps the best souvenir ever: the skills to cook Thai food at home.

Going alone or with a friend? This is a great way to meet new people as each class is an intimate group of 4-6 people.

How Much: $60 USD / 2000 baht

Muay Thai Fights

Blood, sweat and beers – that's what you can expect with a night at the matches. Sometimes children fight and sometimes adults fight. What's important to remember is that Muay Thai is a respected sport, not some barbaric death match. Locals come to bet on matches and fighters have been training for months to get their turn in the ring! Some nights, the crowds are wild and some nights you practically get the whole show to yourself. Don't expect a Las Vegas show, but a wild view into Thai Culture!

Krabi Town Price: Ringside for 1,800 baht OR Open Stadium seating for 1,200 baht. They both give you a great show – just stick with your budget.
Railay Price: 100 baht – but the show is less professional and more about drinking beers and cheering the fighters on.

You can buy tickets at the stadium on fight night, from a tour office or possibly, from your hotel.

The Best Tours

Krabi Sunset Cruise

The best day you'll have in Krabi – this 5-island Sunset Cruise is your one-stop-shop to make new friends, snorkel with colorful fish, jump off the rooftop of a pirate ship, kayak or paddle board while the sunsets, and swim with glow-in-the-dark bioluminescent plankton in pitch black water. Or...don't do any of that. You can just chill on the rooftop tanning and drinking beers all day, too. Do as little or as much as you like. The tour includes pick up from Ao Nang or Railay AND a really yummy Thai dinner – suitable for both carnivores and vegetarians. This is a day you'll never forget.

Pro Tip

Not a confident swimmer? This is the best tour for you, girl. Michael, the cute Aussie Boat Captain, will drag your ass around using an inflatable tube that you can hold onto while you snorkel safely. He's a freakishly strong swimmer and there is also a crew of Thai guys who can help you in and out of the water.

When: Everyday 1pm-8pm
How Much: $80 USD / 2,600 Baht - Includes dinner, pickup, drop off, snorkel mask, flippers, kayaks, paddle boards, snacks, drinks, and dinner.

The 4-Islands Tour

Everywhere you look, you'll see the "4 Islands Tour" being offered. This tour takes you to the most desirable Krabi beaches and islands with unspoiled white sand islands where you can hop off and snorkel with spectacular sea life. The tours are led by Thai people, so there's not social element or informational angle – rather an opportunity to visit some gorgeous sights and take photos that will make all of your friends jealous.

Price: Starting at $30 USD /1000 baht

Mangrove & Cave Kayaking Tour

Explore a maze of mangroves, caves, and jungle via kayak! The laziest way to get into nature and sightsee, these guided tours feel super relaxed as you glide over still water channels with barely any current at all- just a little paddle navigation required. If ever there was a time to try kayaking for the first time- this is it, sister! The mangrove tours are half-day tours that include hotel transfers, snacks, and some swimming! If you're in the mood for a crazier adventure, there are full-day tours over slightly more challenging routes, as well. Check out Sea-Kayak Krabi or Krabi Cavemen for options!

Price: Tours from $30 USD / 1000 baht

Markets & Shopping

Ao Nang Road
The main road that leads outlines Ao Nang Beach and stretches up towards Krabi Town is filled with shops and stalls selling everything under the sun! Cute bags, dresses, jewelry, oils, soaps – you name it. There is also beach gear like snorkels and Dry Bags to keep your phone safe from sand and water. Just be sure to haggle! You can always get a cheaper price.

Krabi Town Walking Street Market
The mecca of shopping, culture, eating, and drinking- Krabi Town Walking Street should not be overlooked! This is your chance to peruse over 50 stalls selling handmade treasures like chic leather purses, sparkly sandals, and cheesy 'Krabi' t-shirts and tank tops. Eat while you shop with stall after stall of sweet and savory Thai treats.

Open: Friday - Sunday from 5pm – 10pm
Location: Soi Maharaj 8 - behind Vogue Department Store

Krabi Nightlife

Ao Nang

You'll find tons of laid back beach bars all along the Ao Nang strip, some clubs in Ao Nang Center Point, and if you want to do some epic people watching, visit Soi RCA where men go to find "intimate company" for the night. All areas are well-lit and busy with tourists from all walks of life. Also! There is a Krabi Pub Crawl that tours around every Monday, Wednesday and Friday with Slumber Party Hostel for 450 Baht.

Railay Beach

Let's be real, your cocktail hour will probably begin at 3pm. If that's the case, start at **Bamboo Bar** for a cold beer, then hop over to **Jamaica Bar** or **Black Pearl** for live music in the evening, and then walk over to Railay East for **Why Not Bar** and **Last Bar** at night where there is Muay Thai and Fire Dancing. You can also join the **Railay Pub Crawl** which is pretty small in terms of bars but throws you into an instant social situation for the night!

Tonsai Beach

The party scene here is definitely happening…but with more of a trippy 60's "hippie" influence, if you catch my drift. There is fire dancing, reggae music, dance parties- all of it. If you plan to partake in hippie activities, stay the night at a guest house on Tonsai.

Which brings me to my next point which I cannot stress enough!

At night, only party on Tonsai Beach if your accommodation is on Tonsai Beach. Once the sun starts to set and the tide comes up, it is extremely difficult to get back to Railay in the dark, especially if you are a bit buzzed or have been partaking in party activities.

How to Get Around Krabi Town

Walk
Krabi Town, Ao Nang, and Railay/Tonsai are all walkable! You could go your whole trip and not take any public transportation if you bring the right pair of shoes and some sunscreen.

Songthaews
Just like in the rest of Thailand, you can flag down a Songthaew, tell them where you're going, and jump in the back. Press the little buzzer button if you want to hop off early. Most Songthaew rides in Krabi town will cost 20 baht.

Longtail Boats
These classic Thai Longtail boats are waiting at practically every beach to take you on a day tour, to the islands, back to the mainland, etc. Consider them private water taxis.

From Ao Nang to Railay (and vice versa), tickets are 100 baht per person. In Ao Nang, there is a bright yellow kiosk at the bottom of the hill next to the beach where you can buy your ticket.

The boats wait for 8 people to buy a ticket before they set sail – sometimes you can wait 5 minutes and sometimes 20 minutes. Want to rent the whole boat and get going? 800 baht will do it.

To head back from Railay to Ao Nang: Head to Railay East where you can buy a 100-baht longtail boat ticket for a Tourist Kiosk or hang at the entrance to the pier where you can directly pay one of the boat drivers.

To head back to the Airport from Ao Nang: Every Tourist Kiosk offers a 150 Baht Airport Shuttle. You can book same-day!

How to Get to Krabi Town from Phuket

Flying into Phuket first. Heading to Krabi second.
It's an easy route and you've got options.

Option 1: Ferry Boat
There are multiple ferry companies leaving at multiple times throughout the day. Check out the boat time tables at the back of this book.

How Much: $30 USD / 1000 Baht
How Long: 4 hours one the boat + transfers from the pier & your hotel

Option 2: Private Taxi
A private taxi can pick you up anywhere – any time and get you to Krabi on your schedule.

How Much: $70 - $100 USD
How Long: 2.5 hours
For Booking: KiwiTaxi.com or 12Go.Asia

Option 3: Minibus
Go to any tour agency in Phuket and tell them you want a minibus to Krabi. They'll set you up right away with a minivan that goes from hotel to hotel picking up passengers. Sometimes you will wait 30-minutes and sometimes an hour. I suggest booking this a couple hours or even a day ahead of time.

Don't be alarmed if the minivan takes you to a bus station where you switch vans – they are just optimizing their trip to get a full van.

Good to Know
The minivans drive pretty crazy and have you holding onto the "oh shit" handle – but crashes are rare. Getting car sick, that's a different story.

How Long: 3-4 hours
How Much: $13 USD / 450 baht

Option 4: Public Bus
How Long: 4.5 hours
How Much: $4.50 USD / 150 baht

Hire a taxi to take you to Phuket Bus Station where you can catch the Krabi Public Bus. The bus leaves every hour. Just know that when you arrive in Krabi, you'll be dropped off at the Krabi Town Bus Station – 7.5 miles away from the beach.

The public bus is fine if you've packed light and have a Thai Sim Card or International Data. You'll need to do some navigating from the Krabi Bus Station to your hotel. OR just download "Krabi Google Maps Offline" and you can show your hotel location to a tuk tuk driver when you arrive.

Super Pro Tip

If you're on a really tight schedule but want to see Koh Phi Phi or Koh Yao – you can take a ferry from Phuket to either of those islands first.

Koh Yao – you can stay the night and take a morning ferry to Krabi. Koh Phi Phi- You can stay the night and take a morning ferry OR you can do a quick 4-hour stop over to explore Koh Phi Phi and head on your merry way.

Just arrange your ticket to Krabi before you go exploring

Extra Super Pro Tip

If you're taking a private taxi, there are two temples along the way that are almost completely unknown by western tourists:

Wat Suwanna Kuha
Also known as Money Cave Temple, you'll wander into a cave where you'll find this opulent reclining buddha under limestone rocks.

Wat Bang Riang
A hilltop temple featuring the Chinese Goddess of Mercy and the Golden Meditating Buddha – both with a stunning jungle backdrop.

Pay your driver an extra $10-20 and viola – you've just created your own day tour.

Getting into Krabi Town

Note: Going to Railay Beach or Tonsai Beach? Get to Ao Nang first. From there, you can hop on a long tail boat that will take you to Railay Peninsula for 100 baht per person.

If you're getting in late, stay in Ao Nang Beach – water taxis to Railay Beach are scarce after 8pm (particularly in low season).

From Krabi International Airport

Krabi Airport is tiny. This is great for you! It means less time spent inside the airport and zero chance of getting lost.

The airport is 9 miles from the Krabi Town and 24 miles from Ao Nang. Expect to take about 45mins – 1 hour to get from the airport to your destination. It sounds like a long ride…but the drive is beautiful!

Option 1: Fixed Rate Taxi
There are no metered taxis at Krabi Airport- only fixed rate. Prices can vary but the below prices are a good reference.

Where: You will find taxi booths inside the Arrivals Hall
How Much: (give or take 100 baht)
 ❖ Krabi Town – 400 baht
 ❖ Ao Nang – 500 baht
 ❖ Had Yao – 800 baht
 ❖ Railay Pier (boat included) – 700 baht

Option 2: Airport Shuttle Bus
Where: You can buy tickets at the same place as the taxi booth inside the Arrivals Hall. Go out of the arrival doors (you'll still be inside the airport) and make a left. You'll see a sign for "Shuttle Bus".

How Much:
 ❖ Krabi Town- 100 baht
 ❖ Ao Nang – 150 baht

When: The Shuttle Bus leaves 8-10 times between 8am-8pm (so almost once per hour). Once you get your ticket, you'll go outside of the airport and see a big white bus. Most travelers take this bus, so the staff are attentive and will guide you in the right direction.

Option 3: Pre-Booked Private Transfers

Book ahead of time with YourKrabi.com and have a car or minivan waiting to take you to your hotel.

Hotels in Krabi Town: minivan - 800 Baht
Hotels in the Ao Nang area: minivan - 800 Baht
Hotels in Koh Lanta: minivan - 2500 – 2800 Baht, depending on where on the island you are staying.

Option 4: Songthaews to Krabi Town

Where: Walk about 400 meters to the main road and flag down a public Songthaew.

How Much:
* Krabi Town- 30-50 baht

When: 6am-11pm (roughly)

From Krabi Bus Station

Option 1: Songthaews to Krabi Town

Where: You'll see brown and white Songthaews once you step off the bus. They each go in different directions- so show them where your hotel is located on a map or tell them the name of your hotel. The driver will let you know if they are going in your direction. Keep asking until you find one to invite you on board.

How Much:
* Krabi Town- 20 baht
* Ao Nang- 60 baht (White Songthaew)

When: All bus hours

Option 2: Metered Taxi

Where: You'll see taxis once you step off the bus.

How Much:
* Krabi Town- roughly 100 baht
* Ao Nang- roughly 150 baht
* Anywhere else you'd like to go- just make sure they run the meter.

When: All hours that buses arrive

Chapter 4: Koh Yao Noi & Koh Yao Yai

You wanted a secret island? I'll give you two.

Imagine Jurassic Park with giant monitor lizards crossing dirt roads and jungle huts and eco resorts that buzz with wildlife as soon as the sun goes down…but less scary and with comfier beds.

Nestled off the coast of Phuket in Phang Nga Bay – here is your chance to get off the beaten path without venturing too far from the mainland. Koh Yao Noi has the most beautiful beaches while Koh Yao Noi offers stunning inland landscape with lots of jungle.

So how has this twin gem managed to stay so hidden? We have the 90% Muslim population to thank for swatting the party bars and backpacker hostels away like flies. Don't worry, you can still find alcohol and a few bars on Koh Yao Noi & Yai, but never will you find a pub crawl or a full moon party.

This is a simple set of islands. One where it's easy to disconnect – not because they don't have internet…they do. But because you can fall asleep to the sound of crickets rather than house music and spend your days getting to know the locals rather than the tourists.
Just a 10-minute long tail boat ride between the islands, give them both a little love.

Koh Yao Noi – Breakdown

The Very Northern Tip

Straight up green on every map, this jungley territory doesn't seem to have a name in English – and I kind of like it that way. This mysterious area is dense with jungle and lined with red dirt roads leading to your accommodation. Peaceful during the day. Glittering stars at night.

East Coast

Most of the guest houses on Koh Yao Noi are found on the east coast, where you can wake up to views of the incredible limestone islands of Phra Nang Bay glittering in the distance. Here's how we can break the East Coast Down:

- ### Upper East Coast

Some of my favorite guest houses are on this beach overlooking the limestone islands of Phra Nang Bay. You're far away enough from other guesthouses that you have privacy, but close enough that you can jump on a bike to try a new restaurant for lunch.

- ### Khlong Jark Beach

Fancy resorts with infinity pools, welcome drinks, and jasmine-scented towels – that's what you'll find sitting on the white beaches of the Lower East Coast of Koh Yao Noi. Rooms average at about $300 USD per night, also with stunning views of Phra Nang Bay. Because Koh Yao Noi isn't yet on the tourist radar, you often enjoy star treatment with a favorable staff-to-guest ratio down here.

- ### Pasai Beach

Don't be thrown off by the words that I'm about to say: at Pasai Beach, you'll find "budget accommodation." Meaning that rooms are simple, and prices are cheap – but adventure is not far away. Just below the Khlong Jark Beach is Pasai Beach – home to more locals and chickens. Plan on making friends.

Koh Yao Noi Town/Village

Exciting news! There IS a 7-Eleven on Koh Yao Noi! You can have toasties everyday…or enjoy the cheap and local Thai food – where the locals actually eat! Koh Yao Noi Town is nothing more than a couple blocks of paved roads and a few government buildings, but the people there are incredibly kind and welcoming. You're just a 5-minute scooter ride away from jungle and beach life, too.

The Hideout Secret Beach

The southwestern peninsula that looks like a little tail? That's "The Hideout" or "Secret Beach." It's a private beach owned by the glamorous Hideout Tree Houses that are such a splurge but a once-in-a-lifetime bucket list kind of deal. You can always hop on a motorbike to come have lunch or dinner in their restaurant and then explore the beach yourself. Just message the resort first and make a table reservation so they know that you're coming!

Inland Jungle

Get your ass in there. A maze of red dirt roads and palm trees offers you the chance to remember what it feels like to be human. Reconnect. Just bring bug spray.

Koh Yao Yai– Breakdown

Koh Yao Yai may be bigger, but half the island is rocky terrain –
which makes for a beautiful getaway, but there are actually less places
to stay on this map than the other…

Because this island is so uniquely shaped, I'm going to break it down
in the easiest-to-understand way, only highlighting the areas that will
matter to your trip.

The Shrimp Head (The North)

When looking at the map, tilt your head to the right and you'll see it.
The whole northern half of Koh Yao Yai looks like a giant shrimp
head. Dense with jungle and lined with a few beaches, this is the
ultimate exploring territory.

- **Pet Nam Bay**

The very norther tip of Koh Yao Yai is similar to the smaller island in
that it's a damn pretty place to explore with lush greenery and Laem
Had Beach – but no accommodation.

  o **Laem Had Beach**

The most beautiful beach on Koh Yao Yai, Laem Had Beach has a
really unique feature: a pure white sandbar that jets out into the
crystal blue ocean. The sand bar is scattered with picturesque palm
trees that are just #TravelGoals to the extreme. To get there, you'll
bicycle or motorbike down a red dirt road – about 15 minutes from
civilization. Bring a picnic. Spend the afternoon here.

- **Klong Hia Pier**

Situated in Chong Lat Bay, Klong Hia Pier connects you to Koh Yao
Noi. You'll find some accommodation and restaurants in this area –
and it's a nice place to stay if you want to venture up towards Pet
Nam Bay via bicycle.

- **Son Bay Beach**

On the neck on the shrimp's head, you'll find one of the only
beautiful beaches on the island! White powdery sand and water that
is perfect for swimming during dry season!

- **Hin Kong Bay**

The biggest bay on the east coast of Koh Yao Yai, this is where you'll
find the best views of Phra Nang Bay. With the most options in terms

of accommodation any budget is welcome with a mix between mid-range and luxury.

The Skinny Waist (The Center)

The very center of Koh Yao Yai looks like a Barbie doll waist – suddenly it's impossibly thin! On the west coast, you have a large bay and on the east coast is Koh Yao Yai Beach.

- **Loh Poh**

The west coast of the waist isn't a place for swimming or sunbathing – rather sunsets and mangroves. There are a couple resorts that have access to beach – but it's not worth your time.

- **Koh Yao Yai Village**

This east- coast village offers a handful of beachfront accommodation and lots of little restaurants. Explore Cape Khlong Bon and the little island right across from it called, Ko Lo Kalat.

- **Koh Yao Yai Beach**

This is the longest beach on the island. It isn't picture perfect and the quality of the sand depends on the season – but there are plenty of worthy resorts here that will give you stunning views of the bay.

The Lobster Claw (The South)

The southern chunk of the island has a unique shape, lined with a few beaches but mostly rocky terrain.

- **Lo Pharet**

Depending on the season, this is the best beach you'll find on the claw! Soft and sandy with beachful views of the sunset!

- **Bo Le Bay**

Home to the popular GLOW Elixir Resort, you can find some sandy spots to chill for the day when you stay at this resort!

- **Phru Nai Village**

Located in the very center of the Lobster Claw is Phru Nai Village with its own hospital, school, ATM (big deal here), and plenty of motorbike exploring potential!

In conclusion – plan on jungle adventures, Lam Haad Beach, and boat trips when you stay on Koh Yao Yai.

Accommodation Koh Yao Noi

Hill House – Koh Yao Noi $

Don't know how to ride a scooter? This is the perfect place to learn. More like a homestay than a hotel, the host family here will take you in like one of their own. Rent a scooter and let Amina or Don teach you how to master the art of motorbiking and then explore the island with the wind in your hair! Each jungle bungalow has a spacious balcony with a plush hammock, perfect for swinging under the palm trees and looking out onto the bay. Breakfast is served with fresh tropical fruit and coffee just how you like it. I promise you…you're not going to want to leave.

Starting at: $30 USD / 1000 baht
Where: Next to Island Yoga

Homestay with Koh Yao Noi Ecotourism Club $

In an effort to build a sturdy bridge between the locals and the newly emerging tourism industry, Koh Yao Noi Ecotourism Club works with 25 local families to arrange humble homestays. You'll have your own little villa with running water and a fan, owned by a local family who will show you the ropes around the island. You'll get a glimpse into the lives of farming, fishing, and how island kids grow up in this region. **Bonus**: every homestay includes breakfast, lunch, and dinner!

Starting at: $30 USD / 1000 baht
Contact: Mr. Bao at dusit999@hotmail.com

Annattaya Holiday Home $

Sometimes you just want some air conditioning on an island and that's okay! This place is clean, affordable and doesn't throw you right into the jungle with lizards and frogs. Instead, Annattaya Holiday Home is situated in the "town" of Koh Yao Noi, nearby a 7/11, some local Thai restaurants, and some of the only paved roads on the island. You're just a 5-minute scooter ride away from the beach – I'd say this is a pretty good compromise.

Starting at: $30 USD
Where: Koh Yao Noi Town

Tabeak View Point $

This place sells out fast! Not because it offers luxury or glamour, I'll tell ya that much. Rather, the rustic stilted huts offer simple beds and dated furniture – but your adventures will be fantastic. Your host is a retired police officer who is eager to help you plan the best island excursions with boat trips, motorbikes, bicycles – whatever you fancy, he's got you covered. Remember, travel is about the experience.

Starting at: $40 USD / 1300 THB
Where: Khlong Jark Beach

Bannsuan Amaleena $$

After a long day of exploring, it's nice to collapse on a big bed in a cool room. Yep, another bad boy with aircon. These brand-new bungalows are surrounded by a gorgeous tropical garden with banana trees and is located next to a little coffee shop called 'Coffee Time' – the perfect combination! Bannsuan is a bit more expensive than Annattaya because of its prime adventure location on the east coast of the island within a 10-minute walk to the beautiful white sand beach facing Phra Nang Bay.

Starting at: $66 USD / 3200 baht
Where: Koh Yao Noi Town

Paradise Koh Yao $$$

Stay on one of the most picturesque beaches on Koh Yao Noi, called Paradise. It's not a secret beach or a hidden beach, but damn it's a pretty beach. Spend the day with wooden tree swings, hammocks and lounge chairs in the sand. Have dinner in a bean bag chateau where you can watch long tail boats putting in and out of the bay or sit at a table by candlelight with your toes in the sand – it's all about the ambiance here. And the rooms. Ugh. To die for with Pinterest-style attention to detail, heavenly beds, and the best part…air conditioning and a big ass pool.

Starting at: $150 USD
Where: The Very Northern Tip

Koyao Bay Pavilions $$$$

Come unwind at Koyao Bay Pavilions- traditional teakwood villas planted in the jungle amongst the palm trees and just steps from a private beach. The beach overlooks the spotted limestone islands of Phang Nga Bay, with the nearest tiny island just a 20-minute kayak paddle away. And my favorite part? A big swing dangling from an old tree, waiting for you to come and sway with the rhythm of the waves hitting the shore. Peace, zen, and privacy.

….not to mention, Koyao Bay Pavilions has some of the best food on the island. Foodies, you'll want to get in on their Banana Flower Salad.

Starting at: $340 USD
Where: The lower peninsula – east coast

TreeHouse Villas - Adults Only $$$$

Ready to knock something off your bucket list? How about a 5-star luxurious bird's nest style tree house with a private plunge infinity-pool overlooking the bay? The circular rooms are decorated as if your Pinterest Board came to life and the staff are straight out of a Disney movie where it just seems impossible to be that cheerful…but when you're on a private island and this is your job, I get it.

Starting at: $370 USD
Where: Upper East Coast

The Island Hideout - Koh Yao Noi Hotel $$$

If the TreeHouse Villas is a bit too expensive, check this place it. Same concept with treehouse villas overlooking the ocean, but with a more rustic feel. For starters, there's no electricity in your room and no wifi. You are truly forced to reconnect with yourself and your surrounds, which include: an infinity pool, outdoor rain shower, private white sand beach, gorgeous food, yoga, and relaxing spa treatments.

Starting at: $320 USD
Where: Secret Beach

Accommodation on Koh Yao Yai

Backpack Hostel Koh Yao Yai $

Come make some likeminded friends at the only true hostel on the islands. Backpack Hostel isn't your typical 'get wasted and party' place. It's more of a 'play card games and adventure together' kind of vibe – which is way more fun. The hostel is brand new with cozy bunk beds, modern private rooms, and hot showers! Best of all, the staff are super hands on, picking guests up from the pier and driving you for food if you've got a craving – just let the dudes on deck know what you need.

Ps. Depending on the season, there are also tents you can rent on a budget.

Starting at: $12 USD
Where: Klong Hia Pier

24 Camping & Bar $

The name says it all! Here is a great place to camp and an even better place to drink! Coming for the day? The circular bar makes it easy to rock up and interject yourself into the social goings on of the day. Instant friendships. Coming for the night? Set up shop in a double-futon tent where you can fall asleep under the stars. No light pollution here! Just rolling hills and river valleys. Tent prices start at $15 dollars for a mangrove view and $18 for a view of the sea in the distance.

Starting at: $15 USD
Where: Northeast Lobster Head, near Santhiya Koh Yao Yai Resort

Koh Yao Beach Front Hotel $

Everyone should experience sleeping in a traditional bamboo hut under a mosquito net once in their lives! You have your choice between simple little bungalows that sit in the rice fields or right on the beach – both with refreshing outdoor showers. Breakfast is more than you'd expect with sausages, eggs, fruit – the works. Plus, the restaurant makes some killer curries for cheap. This is the best bang for your buck when it comes to beachfront living on Koh Yao Yai.

Starting at: $33 USD /1100 baht
Where: Hin Kong Bay

Thiwson Beach Resort $$

Immaculate. The polished Thai bungalows, the gorgeous infinity pool that seemingly spills into the ocean, the well-kept white sand beach – it's all immaculate. The vibes are super laid back here. Bring a book and set up shop with a beachfront lounge chair or hang in the pool with a yummy cocktail. Breakfast is included, and the restaurant has a full menu for when you get hungry. Want to adventure? They've got kayaks and motorbikes for rent.

Starting at: $60 USD **/** 2000 baht
Where: Hin Kong Bay

Koh Yao Yai Village Resort $$

Want to make your friends jealous? Get back at an ex? Break Instagram? Koh Yao Yai makes that so damn easy. Step into the lap of luxury at this full-service resort on Koh Yao Yai. The villas are made for a princess, the massive infinity pool overlooking Phra Nang Bay looks like it belongs in a 5-star resort, the beach is right there, and the tours – omg the tours- take you to all the bucket list spots in the region. Get your camera out. You're going to want to document this.

Starting at: $140 USD
Where: Koh Yao Yai Village

GLOW Elixir $$

Finally, white sand! GLOW offers all the western comforts you're used to along with the tropical island vibes that you came here for. Choose between modern Thai villas, hot tub villas with private balcony, or go for the private pool villa overlooking to ocean. The beach is small but pristine and the water is perfect for swimming. While the other upscale resort, Santhiya Resort, may be fancier, GLOW is less family-friendly which means more pool space for you!

Starting at: $150 USD
Where: Bo Le Bay

Santhiya Koh Yao Yai Resort $$

Possibly the nicest resort on Koh Yao Yai, Santhiya is pretty special with hand-carved wooden bungalows, a waterfall-esque pool and a stunning white beach. The only downside is that Santhiya Resort can get a bit busy – so consider the private pool villas that overlook the ocean. You'll be able to enjoy every second of sunset without interruption. When you're not enjoying the view, check out the spa that offers luxurious scrubs and massages for half the price of back home.

Heads Up: There are multiple restaurants on the property - Saaitara Restaurant is definitely the best.

Starting at: $200 USD
Where: Loh Pared Beach

Where to Eat

Koh Yao Noi Restaurants

Koh Yao Noi may be small, but the local food culture is incredible.

La Sala

A thatched hut restaurant in the middle of a rice field with palm trees swaying in the background – it doesn't get any more local than this. Also local are the catches of the day: crab, fish, squid and more seafood. Everything is gourmet, made fresh to order and plated beautifully. The setting might be rural, but the meals are sophisticated. The manager is a friendly Scottish bloke who can recommend whatever is on special and cater to any dietary needs you may be rockin'.

Open: Daily 8am-3pm & 6pm-9pm / Wednesday just 8am-2pm
Where: Koyao Bay Pavillions, Lom Lae Beach

Pro Tip

La Sala is literally a hidden gem and you'll need some guidance to get here – particularly at night. Nearby the Ko Yao Pavillions on Lom Lae Beach, I recommend trying to find La Sala during the day if you're staying in the area so that you can easily find it at night. Staying up north? Hire a driver and let him find it!

Rice Paddy

No matter the time of day, the views from rice paddy are breathtaking. Perched up on a hill overlook Phra Nang Bay, this is a spectacular spot to enjoy lunch or come for sunset. Enjoy traditional Thai food like Tom Ka or Burmese dishes like Tea Leaf Salad. Rice Paddy buys all of their ingredients from local fisherman and local markets, so be sure to ask what's on special! They can make your food as spicy (or not spicy) as you like it, vegetarian, whatever. This restaurant is super professional, I can't recommend it enough!

Pro Tip

Like super spicy? They do a "Hellish Tom Yam" that is Thai-level spicy. I dare you…

Open: Tuesday-Sunday 1pm-10pm
Where: Southeast Koh Yao Noi
Address: 20/14 Moo 5, Ko Yao Noi

Kaya

There is something very special about the Phra Nang region that I've mentioned before- and that's the Muslim influence. Now, Massaman Curry is a southern Muslim dish and right here at Kaya – is the best Massaman Curry that you'll experience in Thailand; the rest of Thailand is just trying to copy what southerners do best. Finish it off with a Mango Sticky Rice and you've got the perfect island lunch.

Open: 9:00 am -9:00pm
Where: Southeast Koh Yao Noi
Address: Lam Sai, Ko Yao Noi 82160

Pizzeria La Luna

You may be thinking, "Pizza on an island?" and yea…pizza on an island. The chef is Italian, and the ambiance is a breezy tropical oasis. It just works. This is the #1 spot for pizza, pasta, and incredible appetizers! The past is handmade and the woodfire oven is the perfect touch for thin and crispy pizza. And like every proper pizza joint should – they DO deliver to guesthouses and bungalows in the area…for free.

Contact: +66 084.629.1550
Open: Monday – Saturday 11:00am – 10:00pm
Where: Southeast Between Takao Pier and Island Resort – GPS is your friend.

Everywhere

On Koh Yao Noi, you'll find tons of non-descript Thai spots serving real Thai food the way the Thai's eat it! Best for classic stir fry dishes like Fried Rice or Pad See Ew. You can also get out of your comfort zone and try one regional dishes. These are the cheapest places and you never know when you'll find a gem!

(hey, if you find a place you love – tell me so I can put it on my bucket list for this island!)

Koh Yao Yai Restaurants

Odds are, you'll be eating at your guest house or at the small restaurants that surround it. But there are just a few places worth venturing out for…

Ban Rim Nam Restaurant

Pencil this place in as you make your way between the two islands. Located right next to Khlong Hia Pier, here is the spot to try real Southern Thai Food! The Yellow Crab Curry is rich, the fried spring rolls are extra crispy, and all the seafood is fresh fresh fresh! The view overlooking the bay isn't too bad either. Watch the long tail boats putter in and out – take your time!

Open: Daily 11:00am – 9:00pm
Where: Next to Khlong Hia Pier

Odys Cafe

Maybe it's just me…but sometimes when I'm traveling solo, I want to sit down for a full-on dinner but don't want to sit in a fancy restaurant solo. Odys Café solves that problem. You can order the most upscale dishes like Whole Stir-fried Crab and Yellow Curry with Prawns, along with quality cocktails made with fresh tropical fruit – and then enjoy them in a chilled-out setting.

Open: Tuesday-Saturday 1:00pm – 10:00pm **/** Monday 5:00pm-10:00pm
Where: La Pharet Beach

Chill Chill at Pai

Cheap. Simple. Straightforward. Think of any Thai dish that you like: pad thai, pad see ew, spring rolls, fried rice, green curry…the list goes on and they're all here. The specialty at Chill Chill however, are the iced teas! They've got Thai iced tea in every flavor served in a tall glass, perfect for cooling down and filling up after a fun morning adventure.

Open: 1:00pm – 9:30pm
Where: Hin Kong Bay

Food Note

When you stay on Koh Yao Yai, you will wind up eating at your resort or guesthouse. Restaurants are too few and far between!

Highlights & Activities

You wouldn't expect the smallest islands to offer the biggest adventures – but they totally do. The islands are yours to explore.

Rent a Scooter

Driving around the Koh Yaos looks as if National Geographic and Instagram had an island baby! Rent your own bike for the day and go get lost! Make friends with water buffalo, high five barefoot kids, chase some waterfalls, drive under the palm trees for hours – when it's time to head home, ask the locals where to go. They're super friendly and will be happy to see you and help you.

Any guesthouse or hotel you stay at will be able to hook you up with a scooter rental.

Pro Tip

Try to get your hands on a 150cc motorbike for easy island riding.

Go Kayaking

Mangroves or beaches? You chose. Any place that has kayaks also has recommendations of the best nearby spots – many of which are hidden and deserted on Koh Yao! Ask your guest house for some tips or hey, just go exploring and see what happens.

There's also a little island about a mile away from Koh Yao Noi, called Koh Nok. Koh Nok reminds me of a cupcake in that it has everything to offer – jungle and beach – just miniature sized. Rowing can take about an hour, depending on where you stay, so this is a job for two or a job for one experienced kayaker. Heads up: this is a popular lunch time spot for boat trips, so come before or after noon.

Go Scuba Diving

Just a couple miles south of the tip of Koh Yao Yai's Lobster Claw are some great scuba diving spots including an anemone reef, King Cruiser Wreck, and shark point.

Elixir Divers is the #1 dive shop to get Open Water Certified or just do a couple fun dives in the area.

How Much: 10,900 baht for a 2-day Open Water PADI Course

Island Yoga

Peace, kindness, and compassion. Island Yoga is a repeatable yoga retreat with professional yoga instructors from all around the world who guide yoga workshops of every level. Melt away your worries and quiet your mind as you meditate and grow deeper with your yoga practice surrounded by serenity in nature with a large teakwood yoga studio, cool plunge pools, and shared Thai villas. Join in on rock climbing adventures, boat tours, and Thai Chi in-between classes. Go as intense or laid back as you please. It's all about finding out what feels good to your mind and body at Yoga Island. There are no start dates. Jump in whenever.

Contact: ThailandYogaRetreats.com
How Much: Starting at $100 USD / 3500 baht for 3 Days
Where: Right between Upper East Coast and Khlong Jark Beach.

The Healer

For over 30 years, healing guru Dr. Saad has been healing the body, mind, and spirit of locals on the island. Dr. Saad is a blind medical masseuse – which lends to his ability to read your body and energy so that he can heal you with some massage, pressure points, and traditional Thai methods and reflexology.

You can rock up and hope that he's free, or go to his website and make an appointment: Doctorsaad.com

How Much: $22 USD / 650 baht per hour
Open: Daily 10:00am – 10:00 pm
Where: Koh Yao Yai – Dr. Saad's small straw massage hut is located in a field on the southwest side of the Skinny Waste.
Address: Dr. Saad - Blind Massage Healer, Tambon Phru Nai

*Just search "Khao Yao Healer" in Google Maps

The Best Tours

Koh Yao Yai Village Resort Tours

I'll tell ya right now. Koh Yao Yai Village is a resort that has really nailed it when it comes to offering amazing tours. Honestly, just check out their website and you'll find the following tours with all the deets:

- ✓ Island Hopping Tour
- ✓ Snorkeling at Khai Island
- ✓ Sea Cave Canoe & James Bond Island
- ✓ Village Tour
- ✓ Sightseeing Around Koh Yao Yai
- ✓ Mangrove Forest Kayak Tour

I'll expand on these tours a bit below, so that you can get an idea of what these tours entail.

Your guest house might offer similar tours. If so, great. Go for it. But if your guest house doesn't, here is the place I recommend using.

Phra Nang Bay Island Hopping Tour

There are 2 ways to do this trip:

Option 1: Book your trip with a resort or tour company and be put onto a long tail boat with a group of people for the day. The itinerary will be set for you. You'll be taken to some tropical islands and snorkel spots where you can explore. Lunch is included, and you usually leave around 9am. This is a good way to meet other people and save $30.

Option 2: Hire a private longtail boat and create a personal tour of nearby islands and snorkel spots. You can tweak the itinerary to include or exclude whatever you want. When you've had enough snorkeling, climb aboard and go to the next place. This is the best way to avoid the crowds and hunt down the hidden spots, but it can be more expensive, depending on where you book.

With both tours, you'll spend the day visiting a collection of tiny islands - maybe Koh Hong with white butter sand or Panyee Island – a floating village with a small community living over the water. During the trip you can swim, tan, enjoy a coconut on the beach, and eat some local Thai food. Bring some cash for shopping at some of the stops.

How Much: $75 USD – $90 USD / 2500 -3000 baht

Phra Nang Bay Sea Cave Tour

Travel back in time. Literally. These limestone caves and islands are ancient. Hop in a kayak and follow your guide down calm sea channels and under seacave ceilings surrounded by unspoiled mangroves. These mangroves are teeming with wildlife not found in other areas of Thailand; wildlife such as the Wild Hornbill, monkeys, and lizards of all kinds. These tours usually include a longtail boat stopover on Hong Island and Panyee Island, as well. Trips include water, lunch, and transfer. Done and done.

When: 9am-3pm
How Much: $100 USD / 3500 baht

Snorkel Trip

To the Southwest of Koh Yao Yai, there are a collection of 3 small islands that are home to some fabulous coral reefs – perfect for snorkeling.

- ✓ Khai Nok Island
- ✓ Khai Nai Island
- ✓ Khai Nui Island

These three snorkel spots are pretty popular, some of the islands are even outfitted with a mass of umbrellas and lounge chairs during high season.

If you go on a private snorkel tour with a private long tail boat driver, the resort or guest house most likely has some secret snorkel spots of their own. Just tell them you want to get away from the crowds and they can suggest the best places!

How much: Usually $75 USD / 2500 baht
How Long: 4-5 hours

Spend the Day with a Fisherman

In Koh Yao, the local economy is heavily dependent on fishing and farming. You know, old school. A fun way to spend the day is to hire a local fisherman to take you fishing. You get a special glimpse into the life of a true island local with a fresh seafood BBQ and he gets to enjoy the day with a guarantee of money in his pocket (a luxury that fisherman don't always have).

When staying at a guest house, this is easy to arrange as there are local initiatives that have become welcoming this kind of tourism. Your host will have local connections or will put you in contact with Koh Yao Noi Ecotourism Club. Staying at a resort, however, this might be more tough as the staff are likely not from Koh Yao.

How Much: Offer between 1,500-2000 baht for the day
Contact: If your guest house is out of the loop, contact Mr. Bao at **dusit999@hotmail.com** to be connected with Koh Yao Ecotourism Club.

How to Get Around Koh Yao

Motorbike

The most popular and convenient way to get around the islands is to rent a motorbike for around 250 baht per day. With near-empty roads, you have plenty of space to practice your driving. Some roads are paved and some roads are just bumpy dirt roads. Take your time and enjoy the view.

Bicycle

Still not comfortable on a motorbike? A few guest houses rent bicycles - perfect for small adventures.

Songtheaw

From the pier to your hotel or vice versa, songthaews are always zipping around the island. You can flag one down in town or have your guest house ring one up to come collect you.

Car

It's not uncommon for a guest house host to drive you to the pier or to your next destination.

How to Get to Koh Yao

You're going to take a boat (obviously) but you've got a few jumping off points to choose from!

From Phuket

Head to Bangrong Pier where you'll jump on a long tail boat. Boats leave about every 45 minutes between 8:00am-5:45pm.

How Much: $6 USD / 200 baht
How Long: 30 minutes
When: 8:00 am – 5:45pm

From Krabi

From Krabi's Tha Len pier, you can choose either the speed boat or slow boat to Koh Yao Noi. The slow boat is a fun experience – you pile in with locals and get to experience day to day Thai life.

How Much: Slow Boat for $4 USD / 120 baht or Speed Boat for $6 USD / 200 baht
How Long: 20 minutes or 1 hour
When: 8:00 am – 7:00pm

From Koh Lanta

Head to Koh Lanta Saladan Pier and catch bumpy speed boat to either Koh Yao Noi or Koh Yao Yai.

How Much: $45 USD / 1500 baht
How Long: 1.5 hours
When: Daily 12:30 pm

From Koh Phi Phi

It's a bit of a journey from Koh Phi Phi but nothing you can't handle with some headphones.

How Much: $45 USD / 1500 baht
How Long: 2.5 – 3 hours
When: 11:15am

Pro Tips

Bring Cash

ATMs are sparse. In terms of spending money, I'd say bring 1000 baht per day, if you plan to live modestly. Double it if you want to go to some of the better restaurants on the islands or go on boat trips. When you run out of cash, you can always drive to the nearest ATM with a big of local guidance.

Bring Mosquito Spray

When you stay in the jungle, bugs are just part of the deal. A few spritzes of repellent will do wonders – especially at night.

Say 'No' to the Elephant Park

You might be offered a trip to Phra Nang Elephant Park – don't go. This isn't an elephant sanctuary. It's an elephant prison where the animals are forced to work by entertaining tourists. There are only two ethical elephant parks in the south, and they are both in Phuket. Check out the Phuket Highlights section for details.

Chapter 5: Koh Lanta

Calling all mermaids, Koh Lanta is where you come to become one with the ocean and all of its creatures! Approximately 4 miles wide and 19 miles long, Koh Lanta is the perfect size for exploring and relaxing. Less popular than other tourist destinations, you can expect more unspoiled beaches, less tourists and insanely colorful underwater marine life.

Koh Lanta may not be as developed as the other islands in Thailand yet, it's undoubtedly one of the most beautiful places to visit. It has modern amenities that will let you live comfortably and natural island adventures to turn you into an island girl. You'll never run out of cool experiences to try and beautiful spots to see!

The Beaches of Koh Lanta

In the 80s, Koh Lanta was totally unplugged. It was only in 1996 when electricity was hooked up. Today, there are several comfortable accommodations on the island, electricity is consistent, and there is wifi. Koh Lanta's coastlines have several charming beaches every traveler should visit. The majority of the action happens along the sandy west coast – but don't be afraid to get off the beaten path.

Klong Dao Beach
You'll find quite a number of hotels and resorts at Klong Dao Beach. Surprisingly though, the place isn't that crowded, and they have accommodations that would fit all budget. This beach is also the closest to Baan Saladan Village, a place where shopping outlets, banks, dive shops, a medical center, and local market for souvenirs are located. The village is also where the tourists arrive.

Nearly 2 miles of fine white sand greets you at Klong Dao Beach. The breathtaking sight is enough to de-stress and rejuvenate your soul. You can chill at the beach, take a quick dip in the swimming pool, go to a spa, or have a few drinks at a bar. Don't forget to take lots of photos with the beach and beautiful trees as the backdrop!

Klong Khong Beach
Klong Khong is where the parties are at! You'll find tons of little beach bars and music humming every night. The beach however, is quite rocky so don't expect to frolic in the water.

Albeit less developed, this beach has the friendliest locals and is more peaceful and serene. Most of the accommodations are family-owned and affordable. Klong Khong Beach has a 3-kilometer stretch of gorgeous white sand and lots of palm trees. Head out to a couple of bars in the area, have a few drinks, or watch some fire shows.

Phra Ae Beach or Long Beach
Unlike most beaches in Koh Lanta, Phra Ae Beach doesn't have offshore reefs – which makes this the best swimming beach! The Casuarina trees also provide excellent shade during extreme hot days. The waters at Phra Ae Beach are clean and reasonably deep. And they have amazing sunsets. This place has a combination of budget and high-end hotels. Most of their visitors are from the younger crowd and families.

Klong Nin Beach

At Klong Nin, you can relax on the beachfront restaurants and bars. If you're traveling with families or a group of friends, stay in one of their really fine villas. You won't regret the breathtaking sceneries. Also, at the west end, you'll find Klong Tob, a small secluded area ideal for people who want privacy. Klong Nin is about half an hour drive from the main village.

Kantiang Bay

The spectacular reefs and marine life at Kantiang Bay are a haven for divers. By far they have the best dive spots in Thailand. You can enjoy a laid-back island life here as you relax on the beach with the tropical rainforest as the background. Kantiang Bay is the most popular with the backpackers for it's a cool place to de-stress and chill. This place only has a few family-owned hotels and a couple of high-end resorts too. Overnight camping or a Thai cooking lesson are also great ideas when you're at Kantiang Bay.

Other Spots Worth Mentioning

Lanta Old Town

Decades ago, Koh Lanta's Old Town served as the main commercial port for the island where Arabic and Chinese trading vessels sailed and delivered goods. Some of those merchants stuck around to create the culturally diverse Old Town where you can shop, eat, and sightsee with Chinese and Muslim influence.

Also called Sri Raya, the old town is a seaside village that houses a town center. You've got to see the village here - built with stilts and overlooking the ocean. There are only a few restaurants and accommodations here which means you can explore the Old Town in a short time.

The Southern Peninsula

This is that "off the beaten path" adventure I was talking about. The southern end of the island has several tiny – but gorgeous – beaches, along with stunning waterfalls. You may also want to take an easy trek down to the waterfall located at Klong Jark Beach. If you still have time, visit the Koh Lanta National Marine Park that houses the beautiful Koh Lanta lighthouse. Other spots include great snorkeling sites such as the Ko Maa and Ko Chuek. You can also try cliff diving if you're daring enough!

Accommodation in Koh Lanta

Slacklines Hostel $

Photo Credit: Slacklines Hostel

You might plan on staying one night, but odds are that you're going to fall in love with Slacklines' welcoming energy, sense of community amongst travelers, and its playground property. There is a big pool with a slackline to goof off on during the day and party cabana where travelers gather in the night. Oh, and you're just a quick walk to the beach!

Style: Dorms & Private Villas
Starts at: $10 USD/ 300 baht
Where: Phra Ae Beach
Address: 482 Moo 3 Long Beach, Koh Lanta

Chill Out House $

Remember when you were little, begging your dad to build you a treehouse? Chill Out House is finally answering that dream for you. The hostel is literally built into a tree, creating the most nature friendly vibe you can imagine. Guests love the nostalgic feel, claiming it's what traveling used to be about. You know, before everyone was doing it for the 'gram.

139

Style: Dorms and Privates
Starts at: $9/296 baht
Where: 3-minute walk to long beach
Address: 237 Moo 3, Sala Dan, Ko Lanta District

Hub of Joys Hostel $$

The staff at Hub of Joys Hostel seem to have taken the name a bit literal, because they always seem to be smiling, happy to help you with everything. Unlike the classic corn flakes and sliced white bread hostels are known to serve for breakfast, you'll be treated to fresh muffins when staying here. This isn't the place for supreme privacy, as dorm rooms are the only option, but you're sure to make friends and adventure buddies in the well-designed common areas.

Style: Dorms
Starts at: $19 USD/ 626 baht
Where: 2 miles from Saladan Pier
Address: 341/6, Moo.3, Saladan, Lanta

Sincere Hostel Bar and Bistro $

Right next to the pier and walking street, Sincere Hostel is such a convenient location especially if you're leaving the island early or coming in late. The lounging deck is a pier itself where you can dangle your feet over the water and clear your mind. It's a great start and end to any Lanta holiday.

Style: Private Rooms
Starts at: $24 USD/ 800 baht
Where: Sala Dan Pier
Address: 150 Moo 1, Saladan, Koh Lanta

SER-EN-DIP-I-TY $$

The friendly Thai owner of Serendipity is an ever-present figure at his beloved hostel where he personally welcomes his guests, gives them great tips for navigating the island and provides warm Thai hospitality that you won't find at big hotels. You're a 2-minute walk from restaurants and markets in one direction, and a 2-minute walk from Long Beach in the other. What's not to love?

Style: Private Villas
Starts at: $50 USD/ 1700 baht
Where: Phra Ae Beach
Address: 482 Moo 3 Long Beach, Koh Lanta

Coco Lanta Eco Resort $$

Whether you're seeking a quiet vacation to become one with nature, or you want to remind yourself how fabulous you are, Coco Lanta Resort has what you need. The bungalows located directly on the beach are actually the cheapest option. Can you say major budget win? If you spring for the air-conditioned rooms, you won't regret it. The bathrooms are like a bonus room, perfect for pampering.

Style: Privates
Starts at: $69/ 2,273 baht
Where: Near Lanta Secret Beach
Address: Sala Dan, Ko Lanta District

Alama Sea Village Resort $$$

If it's luxury you're looking for, here it is. Alama Sea Village Resort has everything an island princess needs: hardwood floor villas, cushioned hammocks, an amazing restaurant and an infinity pool with an insane view of the ocean. Being so high up in the trees, you can also expect lots of monkey sightings!

Style: Private Villas
Starts at: $80 USD/ 3800 baht
Where: Bakantiang Beach
Address: 333 Moo 5, Ko Lanta Yai

Siri Lanta Resort $$$

Every room at Siri Lanta Resort opens up to a small garden, which is such a great way to start every morning. Only a short walk from the main road, or the beach, it is centrally located for exploration and relaxation. If you really want to get to know Koh Lanta, you can rent a motorbike from the front desk for reasonable rates and no hassle. When you're done with your wild adventure, come back to Siri Lanta and slip into the pool. What a perfect day!

Style: Privates
Starts at: $80 USD/ 3,800 baht
Where: 2.5 miles to Saladan Pier
Address: 631 Tambon Sala Dan, Amphoe Ko Lanta

Eco Lanta Hideaway Resort $$$

Get away from the hustle and bustle of the real world with a relaxing stay in a traditional, yet comfortable beachside bungalow. Each bungalow has its own porch, hammock, and wicker walls for an ultra-Thai feel. Surrounded by sky-high palm trees and just steps to the beach- this place is paradise.

Style: Private Bungalows
Starts at: $147 USD/ 4,900 baht
Where: Phra Ae Beach
Address: 535 Moo 3, Tambol, Saladan, Lanta Ya

Pimalai Resort & Spa $$$$

There's honestly too much to do at Pimalai Resort, so you may be disappointed when you're not able to finish your cycling class, private Muay Thai lesson, or play a match at the tennis court. Yes, all of these options are available to you when you book a stay. This is in addition to multiple pools, three restaurants, and a private beach. The place is like its own adventure, tucked away from the tourist traps.

Style: Privates
Starts at: $321 USD/ 10,540 baht
Where: Bakantiang Beach
Address: 5 Krabi, Lang Sod pier - Koh Lanta

Where to Eat on Koh Lanta

Lazy Days Restaurant

I'm sure that when you imagined vacationing on a tropical island, you pictured eating Pad Thai by the beach with a cool beer in your hand as you watch the waves crash on the shore. Well, your dreams have officially come true at Lazy Days Restaurant.

Open: Saturday-Friday 7:30am-9:30pm
Where: Phra Ae Beach
Address: 775 Moo 2, Saladan Sub District, Ko Lanta

Fruit Tree Lodge & Coffee Shop
The Fruit Tree Lodge & Coffee Shop is the perfect escape when you're hungry or hangry. Think nature, trees, yoga and homecooked breakfasts. Come for the fresh Columbian coffee, chai latte, pancakes, eggs benedict, energy balls and granola. It's all healthy, fresh, and the perfect boost of vitamins that you need during your Pad Thai Tour of Thailand.

Open: Wednesday to Monday, 7:30am-5pm
Address: 557 Moo 2, Saladan, Koh Lanta

Phad Thai Rock n Roll

The cheapest and most sought-after Thai food on Koh Lanta can be found at this quirky street side stand. Phad Thai Rock n Roll offers six simple choices: pad thai, fried rice and spicy curry. Nothing too complicated. Just extremely fresh and made the way the food gods intended. Fresh tropical smoothies and exotic shakes complete the experience.

The place is owned by a funky musician named Jeab. As it is quite popular, come early to get ahead of the crowds.

Open: Daily, 11am-4pm, 6pm-9pm
Address: 208 Moo 5, Kantiang Bay, Koh Lantayai

L. Maladee Restaurant

Thai cuisine with a tropical spin- L. Maladee is a must-try spot on Koh Lanta, especially if you love seafood. They've got fresh crab and lobsters still swimming around just waiting to be ordered; shrimp paired with sweet and savory sauces for serious foodies, and the chefs can make just about any dish with fresh squid. Everything here is to die for.

Open: Daily 5pm-10pm
Where: Between Sala Dan and Klong Dao Beach
Address: 535 Moo 3, Tambol,Saladan, Lanta Yai

Kunda Vegan Vegetarian Café

You don't have to live a vegan or vegetarian lifestyle to fall in love with this café. At Kunda, every dish is made from scratch with fresh ingredients full of nutrition, flavor, and love! And after a week or two of salty Thai food, your body certainly needs a clean reboot full of fruits, veggies, and maybe even a healthy dose of chocolate.

Open: Daily 9am-5pm
Where: Klong Khong Beach
Address: 91/16 Klong Khong | Koh Lanta Yai

Surya Restaurant & Bar

Aptly named after the Hindu gods of the sun and the moon, Surya Restaurant & Bar is situated right where the sun sets. With beachfront views and pink skies over head, admire the serenity as you dig into famous Thai dishes and fresh seafood – or combine the two with the popular Deep-Fried Fish with Tamarind Sauce.

AND they also offer vegan and gluten free options.

Open: Daily, 11am-11pm
Address: 111 Moo 6, Klong Nin Beach, Koh Lanta

Greek Taverna

Switch things up a bit with some Mediterranean flavors. This Greek-run beach bar serves all the classics from Kebabs with lamb and Tzatziki sauce to homestyle Mousaka. Portions are huge which makes for great value for money- especially on a traveler's budget!

Open: Daily 10am-10pm
Where: Khlong Dao Beach
Address: Moo 3, House 231, Ko Lanta

Highlights & Activities

Kayaking

Fun Fact: Koh Lanta's mangroves are nearly as big as the island itself. Set out on the still waters for a day of leisurely paddling as you search for wild monkeys and monitor lizards while listening to exotic birds singing in the trees.

Best of all, the channel is so calm that kayaking here feels like you're gliding over a lake. However, if fighting ocean currents sounds fun to you, check out Talaben Sea Kayaking for more advanced adventures.

Starts at: $36/1200 baht
Where: Hotel Pick Up

Go Scuba Diving

Unlike many other islands whose coral reefs have been destroyed by an influx of tourism, Koh Lanta's sea life remains relatively intact. The crystal-clear water offers insane visibility to get up close with rays, sharks, and countless communities of colorful fish.

While the quality of other dive sites in Thailand vary depending on the season, Koh Lanta's waters are warm and clear nearly year-round. This makes the underwater conditions ideal for the caves, pinnacles and drop offs in this spectacular diving region.

How Much: Open Water Courses average around $382 USD/ 13,000 baht

Khao Mai Kaew Caves

Trek 30 minutes into the jungle and climb 20 minutes through a dark cave with bats and spiders. How does that sound? Still reading? Cool.

Located in the center of the island, you'll climb, crawl and duck your way through the Khao Mai Kaew Caves along with your guide. Head lamps will be provided but just know, this is no walk in the park – you're going to break a sweat, girl.

How much: Tours start around $20USD / 600 baht
Entrance Fee: $10 USD / 300 baht if you show up on your own

Lounge on the Beach

Duh. But really, Koh Lanta has some of the most beautiful and most diverse selection of beaches in Thailand. Your Instagram account is about to be on fire with white sand islands and rocky reef coves. Set aside a day or two just to take it slow and enjoy what the island has to offer.

Rent a Scooter

You won't get lost! There's only one big road to navigate the island and this big road has no traffic! Koh Lanta is the perfect place to learn how to drive a scooter and you drive around looking for beaches to play on.

Fun Thai Fact

There are over 35,000 Buddhist Temples in Thailand

The Best Tours

4 Island Tour to Emerald Cave

Rise and shine! A car will be at your hotel at 8am, ready to whisk you away to the pier. You'll spend the day snorkeling, swimming, and beach hopping while admiring the gorgeous limestone rock formations the jet out of the water forming these other-worldly islands.

1st Stop: Koh Chuak where you'll snorkel with colorful school of fish living in the island's thriving coral reef system.
2nd Stop: Koh Mook, home of the spectacular hidden lagoon called Emerald Cave. When the tide is low, you will actually swim through the cave entrance until you reach the hidden white sand beach enclosed by massive cliff walls.
Mini Break: Return to the boat for a Thai buffet lunch on deck.
3rd Stop: Near Koh Kradan – you won't dock on the island, rather you'll hop off the boat into the clear water where you can swim and snorkel.
The Final Stop: Koh Ngai, a tiny mountainous island with rocky headlands, white sand beaches, and thick forests – practically desolate except for a few guest houses. Chill out on the beach and walk along the shoreline before you head back to Koh Lanta.

Starts at: $47/1544 baht
Where: Hotel Pick Up
Available: November to April

Private Boat Tour

There's a company called Lanta Dream and Paradise – they organize the most amazing private boat tours, get you away from the crowds, and take you off the beaten path.

Hire a boat for the day and you'll discover tiny islands with unspoiled beaches and warm turquoise waters. They'll provide snorkel gear so that you can explore the reefs around quiet islands like Ko Rok Nok and Ko Ha where there's often not a soul in sight. They also do camping trips! They organize your whole set-up on remote islands like Koh Kradan! Pricey but a once in a lifetime experience.

Starting at: $227 USD / 7500 baht
Check Out: LantaLongTailBoat.sitew.org

How to Get Around Koh Lanta

Motorbikes

The #1 best way to get around is with a motorbike. Similar to motorbike rentals all across the country, expect to spend around to $9 USD / 300 baht per day to rent a scooter. If you are staying a long time, try your luck negotiating the rates for multiple rental days.

Koh Lanta is a great place to learn how to ride a scooter. And if you're going to be a traveler, this is a skill you need! Just wear a helmet and please get travel insurance!

Tuk Tuk

Translates as "three wheels" in Thai, tuk tuks are convenient if you intend to sightsee or just need to get from one beach to another.

How to Get to Koh Lanta

Multiple companies run these boats multiple times per day. Here are the most popular routes. If this route doesn't work for you, check 12Go.Asia or tourist kiosks for more options.

From Phuket by Boat

You'll be picked up at Rassada Pier, make a stop at Koh Phi Phi, and then will be transferred to Koh Lanta.

How Much: $26 USD / 850 baht
How Long: 8.5 to 10.5 hours
When: 8:00 AM & 1:00 PM

From Krabi by Boat

During peak season, November to April, daily ferry boats are available.

How Much: $7.50 USD / 250 baht
How Long: 1.5 hours
When: 11:30 am & 1:00 pm

From Krabi by Minibus

How Much: 12 USD / 400 baht
How Long: 2.5 hours
When: 7:00am – 5:00pm, every hour.

From Koh Phi Phi by Boat

From both Tonsai or Saladan Pier.

How Much: Starts at $14 USD / 450 baht – depending on the company
How Long: 30 minutes – 1 hour
When: Several throughout the day, starting at 9:30am

Chapter 6: Koh Lipe

Divers and snorkelers – it's time to cross Koh Lipe off of your Underwater Bucket List.

This tiny little island off the Andaman Coast is the place to swim with Manta Rays, Sea Turtles, Giant Grouper Fish, Lobster, Eel and even Sharks! The beaches ain't bad either. Actually, it's safe to say that the beaches in Koh Lips are some of the best beaches in the world.

As you know, however, nothing worth it ever comes easy. Koh Lipe takes time to get to and so you'll need to clear at least 4 days out of your travel schedule to visit – 2 of which will be travel days.

Once you're here, it will all be worth it. Koh Lipe truly is paradise.

Island Breakdown

The quickest and easiest island breakdown ever!

Sunrise Beach

Every movie, every postcard, and every dream you've ever had of a paradise island is right here on Sunrise Beach. Baby powder soft sand and warm turquoise water alongside intimate resorts and beach bars tucked into tall billowy trees makes Sunrise Beach heaven on earth.

Pattaya Beach

From Sunrise Beach, Pattaya Beach is just a quick 15-minute walk through Walking Street. Pattaya Beach is where the ferry boats pick up and drop off in high season. Pattaya is the most populated beach in terms of shops and resorts – but make your way to either end and you'll find quiet resorts with plenty of sandy real estate to lay your towel.

Sunset Beach

Sunset beach is a great for activities! You can bicycle to the beach, go kayaking once you reach the beach, watch the fleet of longtail boats putter in and out – and of course, see the sunset. Sunset Beach isn't ideal for swimming– but it's a great place to spend the day!

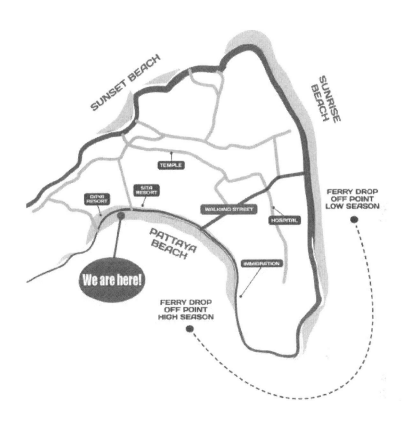

Accommodation in Koh Lipe

Address are no good here. When you get off the boat, just tell a local where you're going, and they'll point you on the easy path towards your accommodation.

Castaway Resort $$

On land and underwater, Castaway Resort is a legend on this island. This resort is what island dreams are made of with big wooden villas overlooking the water and a restaurant where cocktails are complimented with breathtaking sea views.

On top of that, Castaway is the #1 Dive Center on the island. They've got top-notch equipment, small & personal dive groups, and professional staff from around the world.

Ps. When you dive with Castaway Divers, you can get up to a 20% discount per night on accommodation and in low season, some rooms are even free for dive course students– depending on availability. Of course. Check with Castaway before you book your course and your room. You might be able to get a nice bundle deal.

Style: Privates
Starts at: $80 USD/ 2800 baht
Where: Sunrise Beach

Bloom Cafe & Hostel $

Honestly, you may feel like you're cheating when you stay in a hostel like Bloom. It's not the struggle life backpackers are used to. It's a bit too clean, the staff are too kind, and the walk to the beach is just too easy and short for this to really be a hostel. If you're trying to experience the bare minimum hostels are known for, you'll be a little disappointed by the overwhelming comfort of Bloom.

Style: Dorms and Privates
Starts at: Next to Lipe Floating Pontoon
Where: $18 USD/ 593 baht

Gecko Lipe Resort $$

Located along the popular walking street, Gecko Lipe Resort is the perfect spot for exploring as you've got all the shops, restaurants, and bars within spitting distance! When you're done exploring, relax in a traditional Thai hut that will make you feel like a real traveler immersing yourself in another culture. Don't be alarmed by the name; geckos are actually good luck and thought to bring guests good fortune…plus, they eat the mosquitoes.

Style: Privates
Starts at: $48 USD/ 1,581 baht
Where: Next to Lipe Floating Pontoon

Bayview Sunset $$

The scenery surrounding your idyllic wooden cottage is almost too good to be true! You can either melt into the jungle that surrounds you or stay in the sea view cottage with views of the sunset every evening. Both options create a postcard vista right from your balcony. Seriously, this place is just perfection. And if you're still not sold, maybe the thought of eating breakfast with your toes in the sand will do it. The quiet beach is perfect for snorkeling and you're just a 10-minute walk into town.

Style: Privates
Starts at: $54 USD/ 1,779 baht
Where: Lipe Floating Pontoon

AKIRA Lipe Resort $$$

If the fear of visiting Thailand only to drop everything and never return home is a real thing, it's because of places like Akira Lipe Resort. The rooms are set up to look more like small apartments than a stuffy hotel. Come back after a sandy day, take a rain shower and then slide into a pair of house slippers that will make you forget all about the life you've left back home. With an on-site restaurant, bar, and THREE swimming pools, AKIRA Lipe Resort is worth every penny.

Style: Privates
Starts at: $160 USD/ 5,275 baht
Where: Lipe Floating Pontoon

Serendipity Beach Resort $$$$

Tucked away from the touristy areas, Serendipity Beach Resort is the perfect place to experience what the real Thailand is all about. Constructed with traditional teak wood and designed with authentic Thai architecture, staying at Serendipity immediately transports you into a calming cultural experience…and the unobstructed sea views aren't a bad touch, either. If that's not enough for you, go ahead and upgrade to the private pool villa. And if you're the kind of girl who wakes up hungry and in need of coffee ASAP, Serendipity is famous for having one of the best breakfasts on the island.

Style: Privates
Starts at: $333 USD/ 10,971 baht
Where: Lipe Floating Pontoon

Mali Resort Sunrise Beach $$$$

Blanding Thai culture with Balinese esthetic, Mali Resort on Sunrise Beach gives you an Asian fusion experience to remember. The traditional Balinese ceilings featured in every room will make you forget you're in Thailand, until you step out of your suite and see Koh Lipe's famous sunset and white sand beach. The infinity pool is massive with cozy lounge chairs and umbrellas, with pool side service. The restaurant here is also one of the best on the island – but just in case you want to venture out, your resort is within walking distance to a handful of beachside bars and cafes. Paradise.

Style: Privates
Starts at: $303 USD/ 9,983 baht
Where: Lipe Floating Pontoon

Where to Eat on Koh Lipe

On the Rocks Restaurant

Located inside the Serendipity Resort, On the Rocks Restaurant is a 3-tiered dining place and bar which has a terrace overlooking the sea. It's about 800 meters from the Kathalee Beach Resort and the Koh Lipe ferry terminal. Its specialties are Thai and Asian seafood dishes with vegan and gluten-free options. The average cost of meals for 1-2 persons are from $10 to $20. There's a 20% discount on food and drinks during off-peak hours from 4-6pm. They accept major international credit cards. For online convenience, they offer free Wi-Fi access.

Open: Daily 10:00 AM – 10:00 PM
Where: Near Kathalee Beach Resort and Koh Lipe ferry terminal

Koh Lipe Walking Street

One stretch of paved pedestrian road holds nearly all of Koh Lipe's shops and restaurants. There are Seafood BBQ restaurants, international restaurants, and tons of little street-side stalls selling everything from dried squid to sweet pancakes. Eating on this street is inevitable and one of the greatest joys of staying on the island.

Sunrise Beach Restaurant

This beach-front restaurant is known in the island for their Thai and Asian seafood dishes with vegan and gluten-free options. It provides a scenic view for its diners plus free Wi-Fi access. The recommended items on their menu are home-made spring rolls, pineapple fried ride, Pad Thai noodles, their curries and stir-fry dishes. They are paired with their special Thai iced tea. The average meal price for 1-2 persons is $10. The place is clean, and the service staff is friendly and helpful. This restaurant is one of the highly recommended places on the island.

Open: Daily except Saturdays 7:30 AM – 9:00 PM
Where: Near Adang Sea Divers

Cafe Tropical

Healthy food! After a week or so of traveling around Thailand, your body and soul will begin to crave fresh fruit, vegetables and clean proteins! Thank god for Café Tropical. They offer super nutritious meals that give your body a break from the common "fast foods" found in Thailand. We're talking about tropical smoothie bowls, fresh salads, guacamole, cold-pressed juices, and real hand-crafted coffee! COFFEE!

Open: Daily 7:00AM – 11:00 PM
Where: Near Sunrise Beach and Ricci House Resort

Elephant Restaurant

If you are looking for American food, Elephant is the place. This bar/café promotes their special pizzas and burgers. The recommended items on their menu are their home-made Italian Sausage Pizza and their Elephant Burger (don't worry, no elephants were harmed in the making of the burger!) Their coconut pie is also a must-try. Foods are reasonably-priced but their cocktails and alcoholic drinks can be expensive. In the evenings, they have a live band music which you can join in singing your hearts out. If music is not your style, they offer board games while you are waiting for your food to be served. Unfortunately, they don't offer free Wi-Fi access but still, this place is highly recommended.

Open: Daily 7:00 AM – 12:00 MN
Nearest Landmarks: Pattaya Beach and Koh Lipe ferry terminal
Address: 358 Moo 7, Walking Street, Koh Lipe

Bombay Indian Restaurant Ko Lipe

Indian on an Island? Yes! For Indian, Thai and other Asian dishes, head out to Bombay Indian Restaurant. They offer delicious and traditional Indian dishes. The recommended items in their menu with generous servings are naans (garlic, cheese, chicken, butter), mango lassi, samosas, paneer butter masala, and tandooris. Aside from their food, try their drinks and Indian-style desserts. The average price for 1-2 persons is about $10. Their staff's service is warm and friendly. Despite opinions on the great food they serve, there are mixed perceptions of the place's cleanliness.

Open: Daily 11:00 AM – 11:00 PM
Where: Opposite Ricci House Resort, Sunrise Beach

Highlights & Activities

Scuba Diving

Arguably, the best diving in the Andaman Sea is right here off the coast of Koh Lipe. Divers come from all around the world for fun dives, Open Water Courses and to advance their diving skills to become Dive Masters. And if you're going to spend a decent amount of time taking said courses, Koh Lipe ain't a bad place to be.

You'll see...
- ✓ Giant grouper fish, barracuda, sea turtles, sea horses, leopard sharks, blacktip sharks and marble rays

And you'll dive in...
- ✓ Shipwrecks, granite pinnacles and sloping coral walls, and sites with ominous names like "Sting Ray City" and "Stonehenge"

The Best Dive Centers on Koh Lipe: Castaway or Davey Jones' Locker

Snorkeling

At some point, you get tired of boat trips and just want a DIY adventure. Head to the south end of Sunrise Beach for your own private snorkel trip. There is a vibrant coral reef with colorful sea anemones, curious clown fish, glittering parrot fish and even puffer fish!

On your way to Sunrise Beach, pick up some snorkel masks and I highly recommend grabbing some fins as well. Not only do the fins help you glide through the water, but they protect your feet from the reef.

You'll see masks and fins for rent all up and down walking street, and around the island. If no, check out Captain Yut's Huts (50 baht masks) or Castaway Resort (100 baht masks).

Sleepover on Koh Adang

If you stand on Sunrise Beach and look out into the sea, you'll be staring at Koh Adang in the distance. This remote island has just 1 resort. Other than that – there is absolutely nothing here. Sounds tempting already, doesn't it?

Check out Adang Island Resort. Yes, they have an infinity pool…but they also have an entire damn island to themselves. The adventures are endless, and the beaches will leave you speechless.

While you're over there, check out Koh Adang's viewpoint! It's a 30-40-minute hike with a bird's eye view of Koh Lipe's fascinating formation.

Starts at: $74 USD / 2,430 bah

Koh Lipe Nightlife

Koh Lipe Walking Street

15 to 20 minutes is all it takes to walk from one end of this paradise island to its other side via the Koh Lipe Walking Street. It is a narrow blue stretch of road housing several bars, dive shops, massage parlors, pharmacies and restaurants. It comes alive at night with only a handful of shops servicing tourists during the day.

Open: 6pm-12am

Pro Tip

Cash is king on Koh Lipe. Many of the shops and restaurants of the island do not accept credit card – and if they do, they may charge a 3% - 8% transaction fee. It's best to bring cash or go to one of the ATMs on Walking Street.

Fun Thai Fact

Thailand is the world's largest producer and exporter of natural rubber...a substance that comes from trees!

How to Get Around Koh Lipe

Walk

It takes 15 minutes to walk from one beach to the other. No need for cars or tuk tuks here.

Taxi Bike

If you're got too much luggage or just can't be bothered to walk from one end of the island to the other – your resort can call a taxi bike to come pick you up.

Fun Thai Fact

When we go to the cinema in Thailand, we all stand for the King's Anthem before the film begins.

How to Get to Koh Lipe

 From Bangkok / Hat Yai

Step 1: Fly to Hat Yai from Bangkok – with the AirAsia Plane, Shuttle and Ferry Bundle for around $60-70 USD

Step 2: Take a shuttle bus to Pak Bara pier.

Step 3: Take a 1.5 hour boat to Koh Lipe.

To do this smoothly, you must follow this time table:

Air Asia Flight	6:30 am
Shuttle to Pak Bara	9:00 am
Ferry Boat	11:00 am
Arrive in Koh Lipe	1:00 pm

Literally just Google, "AirAsia Bangkok to Koh Lipe" and the package will pop up.

 From Phuket

There are a few ferry companies that run speed boats from Phuket to Phi Phi.

How Much: About $70 USD / 2300 baht
How Long: 5 – 6 hours
When: 7:30am, 8:00am, 8:30am

Chapter 7: Khao Lak

The unspoiled beaches of Khao Lak are one of Thailand's best kept secrets... but not for long.

Located about an hour north of Phuket Airport, Khao Lak is still considered "off the beaten path" for Thailand's tourism industry.

This means that beaches are pristine, underwater corals are thriving and local life still runs at an authentic pace.

Resorts and nightlife have only just started popping up, giving you a glance at what the more popular spots, like Phuket and Koh Phi Phi, might have looked like 20 years ago before the tourism wave it.

But there's more to Khao Lak than just gorgeous white sand beaches. Venture inland and you'll find lush jungles, lakes, and the incredible Khao Sok National Park. Head underwater and you'll discover thriving coral reefs teeming with colorful marine life.

Now is the time to explore Khao Lak. With 12.5 miles of unspoiled coastal territory and only a handful of beachfront resorts, you the best of both worlds: total comfort and total adventure.

At night, Khao Lak is quiet. There are not big party areas, rather a couple holes in the wall and more of a "cocktails and sunsets" vibe.

The best part is that Khao Lak is still considered off the beaten path for backpackers and tour groups – giving you a taste into local life through fresh markets, rural villages, and street vendors galore.

Fun Thai Fact
World-famous golfer, Tiger Woods, is the son of an American father and a Thai mother.

The Beaches of Khao Lak

Khao Lak is the least complicated coastal city to map out. Broken down into three main sections from South to North, each area has its own personality – getting less and less touristy the farther north we explore.

Bang La On

The center of Khao Lak's vacation paradise is actually called Bang La On – but people still refer to it AND its beach as Khao Lak and Khao Lak Beach. Bang La On is a small version of any modern-day Thai city with colorful food stalls, a few western restaurants and tour shops set up everywhere you turn…but somehow with an intimate charm.

That being said, staying in Bang La On is a great idea. Some of the best resorts have set up shop here and for good reason. Everything is within walking distance and the local Nang Thong Beach is absolutely stunning.

Bang Niang

When the center of town is marked by a 7-Eleven, you know this place is tiny. Bang Niang, just north of Bang La On, is less touristy but does have a few attractions to entice you this way!

There is a day market every Monday, Wednesday, and Saturday, from roughly 1pm - 7 or 8pm *and* there's a flicker of friendly nightlife here – more so than in Bang La On.

Khuk Khak

Do you want to see what real day-to-day Thailand is like? Khuk Khak is the base camp for labor workers and fruit vendors who are still not used to the novelty of seeing tourist (lots of smiles coming your way). Come wander the hardware streets and fresh fruit market and eat where the locals eat at roadside stalls for $1.

Want to keep exploring? There are more beaches north of Khuk Khak – but you'll need a motorbike to get there. Here are some extra sandy adventures...

- **Pakarang Beach**

So much room for activities! Pakarang Beach's most notable feature is how much space there is from the jungle line to the shore – and that line stretches unbelievably far when the tide is out. The turquoise water is warm and picks up enough waves for surfing! Keep an eye out for surf board rental stands.

There are also a couple of guest houses up here – so you can pop in somewhere for a bite to eat or decide to stay the night on a whim.

- **Pakweep Beach**

Pakweep Beach boasts an unobstructed long stretch of white sand, ideal for those long walks we've all been hearing about. The perfect place for a beach day with hair braiding stands, cheap bars, and beachfront massages starting at 250 baht per hour! These stands don't litter the beach space, though. They are cleanly tucked towards that back of the beach, keeping Pakweep immaculate!

- **Bang Sak Beach**

The further up you go, the fewer people you'll encounter. In dry season, Bang Sak Beach is idyllic with bath water temperatures and pristine sand. Go exploring. In one direction, you'll find some mysterious jungle paths through palm tree groves and in the other, simple Thai restaurant shacks on the beach.

Accommodation in Khao Lak

No high-rises here - only hidden guesthouses and strategically designed resorts that make you feel one with nature!

Monkey Dive Hostel $

With exceptionally clean dormitories and shared bathrooms, the Monkey Dive Hostel is a step above its competition. Other hostels? Don't even bother! Designed with solo travelers in mind, this hostel has great working spaces as well as fun shared spaces that make mingling easy. In proper hostel form, the bar has an easy menu with items like cheeseburgers and French fries to make you feel right at home. Located in the heart of town, there's no need for a motorbike. The beach is less than a 10-minute walk.

Style: Dorms and Privates
Starts at: $21 USD/ 695 baht
Where: 1.5 miles from Bangnieng Afternoon Market
Address: 7 4/135 Khuekkhak, Takua Pa District

Rakkawan Residence $

Ready to explore? Located in the heart of everything there is to see and do near Khao Lak, you won't need a car or even a motorbike to soak it all in. The beach is less than a ten-minute walkaway, and a grocery store and McDonald's within a stone's throw means you won't have to hunt for a meal. Thai Hospitality is alive and well here – with staff that are more than willing to help plan some adventures for you. It's a convenient location on a convenient budget!

Style: Privates
Starts at: $36 USD/ 1,191 baht
Where: Khao Lak Beach
Address: 4/2 Petchkasem rd. Moo 7

The Herbal Khao Lak $$

Yas, queen. Luxury on a budget is exactly the bargain you've been hunting for. After weeks in dorm rooms and shared bathrooms, the Herbal Khao Lak is a nice change of pace. The private rooms feel more like studio apartments, with small refrigerators and more than enough space for your luggage. Complimentary breakfast is a great way to start your day before relaxing poolside before a day of exploration. This boutique style hotel is the perfect balance of fun and fabulous.

Style: Privates
Starts at: $56 USD/ 1853 baht
Where: Bang Nien Beach
Address: 15 Moo 6 Petchkasem Road, Khuek Khak

Haadson Resort $$$

More of a holistic resort than a fancy one, Haadson Resort is an understated oasis. From the outside, you may think you're in for a more rustic experience, but once your settled in, you'll start to notice the high-end details. Each room is immaculately designed with stunning modern furniture and a clean color palate that looks like it came out of a magazine. Head out of your room, you're just a short, breezy stroll to the beach. Haadson Resort lets you unplug and become one with nature, without sacrificing comfort.

Style: Privates
Starts at: $118 USD/ 3900 baht
Where: Pak Weep Beach
Address: 30/1Moo 7, Bang Muang, Takua Pa District

The Waters Khao Lak by Katathani $$$

Glamourous and luxurious, The Waters Khao Lak is worth every penny. As if one beautiful pool wasn't enough, The Waters Khao Lak boasts SIX swimming pools to splash in – plus a beautiful beach that is only a 6-minute walk away. But when your life is fabulous enough to stay at the Waters Khao Lak, you don't even walk 6-minutes, because the 24-hour reception staff will happily book you a spot on the complimentary beach shuttle to make life easier. Did I mention one of the six pools has a swim up bar?

Style: Privates
Starts at: $125 USD/ 4,136 baht
Where: Bang Niang Beach
Address: 67/238, Moo 5, Bang Niang Beach

JW Marriott Khao Lak Resort and Spa $$$$

When you hear of the Marriot brand, you expect Kardashian-style extravagance. The JW Marriot Khao Lak Resort exceeds even those expectations. Set on a private sunset beach, the JW Marriot has spared no expense in creating the most idyllic vacation getaway that you can imagine with a top of the line restaurant, heavenly spa services, and an infinity pool to outshine all others -there really is no reason to ever leave (except maybe…money). If, however, you decide that the private balcony accompanying your grand hotel suite and direct access to pink sand beaches isn't enough for you, the 24-hour staff will be happy to plan a jungle excursion or island boat trip for you. Staff is impeccable, and you *will* be treated like a queen. Settle into the role, babe.

There genuinely is nothing bad to say about the JW Marriot Khao Lak resort and Spa, unless it's booked up before you've made your reservation…then they suck.

Style: Privates
Starts at: $333 US/ 11,018 bat
Where: Northern Khuk Khak Beach
Address: 41/12 Moo 3, Khuk Khak

Fun Thai Fact

"Farang" is the word for "foreigner" in Thai. It's not a mean word or a derogatory word…although sometimes it is accompanied by smiles and laughter.

Where to Eat in Khao Lak

Siam Turmeric

Siam Turmeric does things a little bit differently 'round here. Take a "Farang" owner from the middle east and give him access to Thailand's fresh seafood, local cuts of meat and organic veggies– and of course he's going to BBQ it all to perfection. Slow roasted pork over a spit roast and massive prawns BBQed and served with the roe; dinner here is an event! Everything is plated beautifully and tropically – perfect to snap a few photos to make your friends jealous. If you want something classic but still adventurous-looking, order the Pineapple Fried Rice.

Open: Daily 10AM - 12AM
Where: Khao Lak
Address: 17/11 Moo 2, Lamkaen

KruaThai

On Pakweep Beach, only about a hundred meters from the shore, you'll find KruaThai – the most popular beachside restaurant for miles. Take your shoes off, let your hair down, and feel the breeze of the sea as you sip on a cold coconut or sweet smoothie. KruaThai is fabulous for the traditional Thai tapas like fried spring rolls, prawn satay, and prawn cakes! Need something of a bit more sustenance? Try the soft-shell crab with tamarind sauce! KruaThai is cheap, consistent, and convenient!

Open: Daily 11.30 AM - 10.00 PM
Where: Pakweep Beach

U-Taro

It may be surprising to learn that a Japanese/Californian fusion restaurant is the most popular place to eat in Khao Lak. Don't fight it, just go with it and visit U-Taro Restaurant near Khao Lak beach.

With a Japanese/Californian fusion restaurant, you can expect all of the sushi rolls from home, plus filling creations using fresh Asian ingredients like tamarind sauce and local seafood. The beer is cold, the sake is imported, and U-Taro does not skimp of filling their rolls to the max. Try the Dragon Roll. You won't be disappointed.

Open: Daily 11:00 AM - 2:00 PM & 5:00 PM - 10:00 PM

Where: Khao Lak
Address: 13/134 Phet Kasem Road

Pam's Restaurant

Excellent food at a great price, Pam's Restaurant cooks up the staples of Thai cuisine with every and any Thai curry with chicken, seafood or vegetables – it's their specialty. **Heads up though:** asking for 'not spicy' in Thailand is no guarantee– especially at such an authentic place like Pam's.

If you want to play it safe, the 'Coconut soup with noodles' and 'Coconut Soup with Rice' are both extremely understated but insanely delicious! Maybe pair a spicy curry and a creamy soup!

Open: Daily 3.00 PM - 10.00 PM
Where: Next to Khuk Khak Temple, on the road going to J.W Marriot Hotel
Address: 60 Moo 3

Qcumber

If you want to eat seafood in front of the sea in Khao Lak, it is a cheap, beautiful and charming place.

To get to this area where, in addition, you can find many other restaurants, we arrive at Khao Lak beach. Here is a quiet area full of hotels (very good looking, by the way) and from where I caught a taxi boat to get to Mae Haad Beach for 200 baht, a highly recommended excursion.

Any curry with meat or vegetables is delicious (I especially like the green in all its varieties, but it is a matter of pure taste), but always itches. Asking 'not spicy' in Thailand is no guarantee of anything. To me their Pad Thai and Mango with Sticky rice were delicious.

Open: Thursday to Tuesday 11.00 AM - 10.00 PM
Where: Khao Lak
Address: 26/22 Moo 7, Phetkasem Road

Highlights & Tours in Khao Lak

Walk through the center of Bang La On and you'll find several tourist shops selling boat tours and inland tours!

Khao Sok National Park

As your longtail boat putters through a green and turquoise maze of stunning limestone mountains and cliffs, you feel like King Kong is going to pop out at any moment. Truly otherworldly, Khao Sok National Park is a *must* when visiting Khao Lak.

Kayak through the emerald green channels of Cheow Lan Dam, hike up to Coral Cave, take a jungle cooking class with a local family, go on a night safari with luminescent bugs... Khao Sok is like being in the Amazon Rainforest...without all the killer animals!

Ps. I absolutely recommend spending a night or two on Khao Sok Lake! There are nearly a dozen floating hotels with bamboo huts literally floating on the water. When you stay here, you can go on jungle treks, kayaking adventures, fishing trips – all of it!

Check out KhaoSokLake.com

Island Snorkel Tours

Off the coast of Khao Lak are some of Thailand's best-preserved islands and coral reefs! Colorful tropical fish, sea turtles, vibrant coral communities – the underwater world is uniquely spectacular in this area of the Andaman Sea. Dive shops and tour centers offer snorkel trips to...

- The Similan Islands
- Koh Tachai
- Surin Islands
- And Koh Phi Phi

You'll hop in a speed boat that will drop you off at different snorkel spots where you'll swim in open water or at nearby beaches and islands. You don't have to be a master swimmer for this trip, either. Life jackets and calm waters make it easy!

How Much: Around $80 USD / 2700 baht
Heads Up: Tours usually run from Mid-October to Mid-May

Scuba Diving
The scuba sites here are insane!

There are shipwreck dives. There are underwater cliffs that drop off unexpectedly. There are boulders and tunnels. It's an underwater playground out and a diver's dream come true.

If you've ever thought of becoming diving certified, Thailand is absolutely the place to get your Open Water certification. Open Water PADI Courses are 4-day courses that throw you in the classroom, then the pool and then the ocean! Dive Masters in Thailand are fully qualified, have tons of experiences and are famously heaps of fun. Plus, how cool would it be to say you got Diving Certified in Thailand?

Even *cooler* is getting your certification on a **Similan Liveaboard**. Basically, you live on a boat, study, and dive in some of the best dive sites in the world.

4-Day Similan Island Liveaboard are available from 15th October to 15th May starting at $770 USD / 25,400 baht

Check Out: Khao Lak Explorer Diving Center
How Much: Open Water Course $350 USD / 11,500 baht.

Markets & Shopping in Khao Lak

TT Plaza – Khao Lak

Get ready to hoard all the souvenirs to bring back home! Situated along Phetkasem Road, right in the heart of Bang La On, TT Plaza is hard to miss. This massive shopping center is a larger-than-life version of a typical Thai market. It covers about 2,000 square meters of space, and you can find practically everything you're looking for, as well as … a lot of stuff that you really aren't looking for.

TT Plaza is a dreamland of knick knacks like elephant keychains, bamboo chopsticks, palm tree magnets and an endless supply of knock-offs covering name-brand electronics, bags, shoes and makeup. You might even want to consider buying an extra duffle bag while you're here to stuff full with new treasures.

Before you head inside to explore the village of shopping stalls, wander the food stalls in front of TT Plaza! Selling Thai snacks like kebabs, pancakes, and corn on the cob – this is a fast way to energize you for the shopping venture to come.

Open: 9am-8pm

Pro Tip

TT Plaza is made of tin and gets really hot inside. Go in the morning before the heat comes and buy a bottle of water at one of the stalls outside.

Khuk Khak Fresh Market

If you're in the area of Khuk Khak, the fresh market is worth a visit and a stroll. Khuk Khak market is a genuine local Thai market. It's small but abundant. The market receives fresh seafood, meat, and fruit every day, summoning locals for their routine of morning shopping and mid-afternoon lunch.

Vendors fry up their famous fried chicken, display pots of colorful, yet mysterious point-and-pick curry, grill juicy seafood, and offer every kind of meat on a stick! Not a lot of English is spoken here, but the vendors here are fluent in pointing, smiles and thumbs up.

Pro Tip

If you're not nearby Khuk Khak market already, don't go out of your way to visit, as you can explore the whole thing in 15 minutes – not really worth a trip. *But* if you're in the area, it's a fun local activity to add on to your itinerary.

When: Early morning to late afternoon
Where: Khuk Khak Bus Station, Phetkasem Road

Bang Niang Day & Night Market

Bang Niang is the oldest market in Khao Lak and holds on tight to local traditions when it comes to food. Vendors will be so entertained to watch you step outside your food comfort zone while sampling Thai favorites like fried bugs and grilled chicken hearts. Stomach not that adventurous? Try some exotic fruit like lychee, mangosteen or the famous stinky Durian! As the sun goes down, more stalls pop up catering to tourists with tank-tops, handbags, and a baffeling amount of usless toys with flashing lights and siren noises. *Why? Just why?*

When: 10am -10pm - Saturday, Monday, Wednesday & Thursday
Where: Phetkasem Road opposite from the Tsunami Memorial Park

Khao Lak Nightlife

Moo Moo Cabaret Show Bar

Have you ever heard of a Ladyboy? Ladyboys are the glamourous and ultra-feminine third gender of Thailand. Come watch the divas of Moo Moo Cabaret Show put on a fabulous performance with extravagant costumes, makeup and choreography. Everything is lip synched, covering all of the famous diva classics from Cher to Brittany. Right at the edge of Bang Niang Beach, the show is free – but once inside, you'll buy cocktails and beers at a premium. Totally worth it for the experience alone. At the end of the show, go take some photos with your new idols.

When: 9:45-11:00pm
Where: Bang Niang Beach
Only Open from October To May Only, Khao Lak, Thailand

Along Phet Kasam Road

While there isn't one designated party area in Khao Lak, the main road is lined with handful of bars and clubs that will keep you entertained (and buzzed) all night.

For the best cocktails, head to Sakai Bar. Want a full on "night out" with House Music and life DJs? BUILD Factor is what you're looking for. There's also Monkey Bar if you want a smaller scene with reggae music and cold beer. You've got options, girl.

How to Get Around Khao Lak

Motorbike
Off the beaten path, the roads around Khao Lak are a lot less crazy and crowded than other places in Thailand. Rent a bike and practice your riding skills. Your accommodation will hook you up with a rental or show you where you can rent. Just wear a helmet and please get travel insurance.

Songthaew
You'll see Songthaews driving around town all day and night. Songthaews are transport trucks where passengers pile in the back like soldiers for a cheap alternative to a taxi. Just wave your hand to flag one down and then tell the driver where you're going – he'll drive you there or you can hop off when you see a spot that you want to explore. Khao Lak Songtheaw prices start at 50 baht and are only are available until 6 PM. After 6pm, the Songthaews suddenly become unofficial taxis and their prices can reach up to 300 baht for a ride.

Hotel or Resort Transport
Want to go to another beach? Check and see if your hotel has transport or free shuttles – many places do! They also often offer airport transfers.

How to Get to Koh Lak

The only way to get to Khao Lak is by road.

 From Phuket

Option 1: Private Taxi
Arrange a taxi to pick you up from Phuket Airport or your hotel – then set off for Khao Lak.

> **How Much:** Around $50 USD / 1,640 baht
> **How Long:** 2hours
> **When:** Anytime when you schedule ahead of time
> **Contact:** Kiwi Taxi, Andaman Taxi or your Khao Lak Resort will likely have a shuttle service for a small fee.

 From Krabi

Option 1: Private Taxi
> **How Much:** Around $85 USD / 2,790 baht
> **How Long:** 2.5 hours
> **When:** Anytime!
> **Contact:** Same as above, love

Option 2: Bus
> **How Much:** Around $10 USD / 300 baht
> **How Long:** 3hours
> **When:** 11:30am
> **Contact:** Phantip Travel

 From Bangkok

A minivan service is available from the airport to Khao Lak!
You can also take the bus from the Southern Bus Terminal (Sai Tai Mai). Be warned, the travel time is quite long.

How Much: Minivan up to $40 USD / 1300 baht; Bus up to $30 USD / 1000 baht
How Long: 11 to 13 hours
When: 6:30 pm

From Surat Thani

A bus leaves from Surat Thani to Khao Lak approximately every 2 hours from 6:00am to 17:00pm. Go into any tour shop and they'll set you up. A tuk tuk transfer to the bus pick up station will also be included.

How Much: Up to $6 USD / 200 baht
How Long: 3 to 4 hours
When: 6 AM to 5 PM

Fun Thai Fact
Elephants in captivity individually chose their human friend. These friends/caretakers are called a Mahouts.

Section 2:

That Random Beach in the Middle

Chapter 8: Hua Hin

Mellow out and melt into local Thai culture in this sleepy beachside town. Located on the central west coast of Thailand, Hua Hin is home to long beaches, adventurous waterparks, and some of the best day and night markets around.

As Hua Hin is only a 2.5-hour drive from Bangkok, it has always been a popular weekend getaway spot for Bangkok residents – the Royals included. Back in the 1920's, Hua Hin was transformed from a low-key fishing village to a royal resort. Nothing too glitzy or glamourous here now (besides a royal residence), but the presence of the royals and high-society Thai vacationers means that you have your pick of restaurants, shopping, and resorts.

While the main beach is a massive 3 miles long – it's not spectacular. The water is clean, the sand is relatively soft and there are snorkel spots nearby; it's just not that white powder sand you've been dreaming of.

Rather, travelers come here to get off the tourist path and get a taste of local life while still absorbing those seaside vibes.

Accommodation in Hua Hin

Buathai Loft Hostel $

Buathai Loft Hostel offers nothing but dormitory options, meaning you'll have more opportunity to meet travelers with shared living spaces. As if that was their intention all along, the hostel is set up more like a second home than typical accommodation options. Past guests rave about the free snacks and water offered to all travelers, saying their experience felt like one with family. If you think I'm kidding, there's even a house cat for the nights when you're super lonely and need a little cuddle.

Style: Dorms
Starts at: $9 USD/ 297 baht
Where: .9 Km to Hua Hin Market Village
Address: 2043 Tambon Hua Hin, Amphoe Hua Hin

Sukkasem Homestay $

Ready to live like a Thai? At Sukkasem Homestay, you're not shacking up in a hotel or a hostel, rather, you're staying in a Thai-style family home located right on the pier! Your room isn't the ritz, but it's comfortable. Some rooms are small, and some rooms have full balconies overlooking the water. Each room gives you a chance to experience true Thai living…but with air-conditioning. The streets surrounding Sukkasem Homestay are always bustling with fresh fruit stands and Hua Hin Night Market is only a five minutes-walk away. And with the amazing location at the pier, you've got easy access to boats for island hopping, snorkeling and kayaking.

Style: Privates
Starts at: $39 USD/ 1,290 baht
Where: .3 Km to Hua Hin Fishing Pier
Address: 21/1 Naret Damsri RD., 77100 Hua Hin, Thailand

Whale Hua Hin Hotel $

You know those times when you're sick of the backpacker options, sharing a bathroom, and you need to remember how fabulous you are, but your bank account only has a laugh in it? Whale Hua Hin Hotel is the place to go in those times. It's just outside of downtown and offers really nice rooms for a reasonable rate. To keep costs low, take advantage of the free city into town, never miss out on the free breakfast, and walk over to the minimart for a few late-night snacks. Let your inner princess flourish without hysterically shocking your checking account.

Style: Privates
Starts at: $54 USD/ 1,786 baht
Where: 1.6 Km to Seenspace Huahin Beach Mall
Address: 32/112 Petchkasem Road Tambon Hua Hin,

The Yana Villas Hua Hin

A beachfront resort with views like this would easily cost you 3x the price back home. But here, off the beaten path in Hua Hin – it's a steal. Besides the obviously incredible infinity pool, the standard rooms at The Yana Villas are apartment-sized with a bathtub, robes, and all the English channels on TV – luxuries that are not standard in Thailand. Feeling fancy? Upgrade your room to a private pool villa and even out those tan lines…if you know what I mean.

Style: Privates
Starts at: $149 USD/ 4,930 baht
Where: .6 Km to Khao Takiap Temple
Address: 122/138, Moo Baan Takiab

Hua Hin Marriott Resort and Spa $$$

There's lux hotels, and then there's Hua Hin Marriot Resort and Spa, a step above everything else. Created like its own tourist attraction, you may be confused to learn this is only your accommodation upon arrival. Don't be shocked if you see a wedding hosted on the grounds during your stay, it's a top choice for destination weddings, and once you're there you'll see why. Everything is straight out of a fairy tale. I'm not making promises, but if you drop a slipper, this looks like the place Prince Charming might hang around. Start your day with breakfast at the renowned restaurant, before spending the day getting pampered with spa treatments like the princess you are. When you're ready to leave the resort, you're in luck because being a guest entitles you access to the private beachfront access just off the massive hotel.

Style: Privates
Starts at: $493 USD/ 16,313 baht
Where: .6 Km to Hua Hin Market Village
Address: 107/1 Phetkasem Road, Hua Hin, TH-77 77110, Thailand

Where to Eat in Hua Hin

DAR Restaurant

If you're looking for a fine dining experience, scratch DAR Restaurant from your list. DAR's laidback ambiance is a far cry from fancy – to the point where you would totally miss it if you were just passing by - but the food here is superb! You must stop in for an authentic Thai meal! Start with a traditional Som Tam Salad aka spicy papaya salad, and then go for some big-ticket items like grilled snapper or the king prawns. Not much of a seafood fan? Try any friend noodle dish here, made in their decades old wok that infuses each dish with a deep aroma and rich flavor that you'll only find in a traditional Asian restaurant.

Open: Daily 1:00 pm -12:00 am
Where: Beside the Main Road, Grand Night Market

Moom Muum Noodle & Rice Café

It's often the most simple-looking Thai restaurants that serve up the most outstanding Thai dishes – and Moom Muum is no exception. This café specializes in about a dozen staple Thai dishes, the kind of Thai dishes that local people eat on the regular, and they make them to perfection. Get out of your Thai comfort zone and order a couple items you won't find back home, such as the Tom Yum Noodle Soup, Massaman Curry or my favorite… Khao Moo Daeng Moo Grob aka crispy pork noodle soup!

Open: Monday to Saturday 10:00 am – 9:00 pm (check first if planning to go on a Sunday)
Where: Located on Soi 94 right across the street from the Narrawan Hotel

Coast Beach Club & Bistro Hua Hin

You may not feel like shelling out hundreds of dollars to stay at the Centara Grand Resort…but you can still vacation like a guest. All are welcome at the Coast Beach Club and Bistro – a brand new beachfront watering hole with creative cocktails, fantastic finger food and must-try mains. Spend the afternoon with your toes in the sand and a class of Prosecco in your hand at one of their sand-tables under the shady palm trees. When the sun starts to set, the beach is lit up with tiki torches, creating a sexy and sophisticated atmosphere for dinner. **Ps.** Happy Hour is from 12pm-2pm!

Open: Daily 11:00 am – 11:00 pm
Where: Hua Hin Beach and within the Centara Grand hotel

Retro Bar & Grill

After wandering through the Hua Hin Night Market, take a break at Resto Bar & Grill. They've got comfort food, live acoustic music and extra friendly service that makes you feel like you're chilling in your friend's bar on a Friday night. The menu offers Thai and American dishes – both of which pair perfectly with a cold beer (Singha is my favorite beer, FYI). Try the burgers or the pizza, soak up the Thai vibes and enjoy the people watching from your barstool perch.

Open: Daily 5:00 pm to 12:00 am
Where: Railway end of the Night Market and Night Bazaar

The Social Salad

The Social Salad is a fresh and healthy restaurant just a few steps away from Hua Hin Fishing Pier. This place is a heaven for fruit juice, shakes, salads (hence the name) and so much more. They've also got plenty of proteins to add in the mix – try the Pork Laab. It's a classic Thai dish that goes well with a fresh salad!

Open: Daily 9:00am-10:00pm
Where: Hua Hin Central

La Terrasse

If you're looking for French or European seafood cuisine with excellent drink selection, consider dining at La Terrasse. Situated within the Hua Hin Beach, the restaurant rests on stilts by the sea and offers a good view of the coast. Although specializing in French and European foods, it still offers a variety of authentic Thai food with generous servings. Recommended dishes to try are their pizzas, glass noodle salad with shrimp, shrimp red curry, spicy fried pork as well as their Tom Yum soup. Their prices are reasonable, the place is clean, and their staff service is attentive.

Open: Daily 2:00 pm – 10:00 pm
Where: Near For Art's Sake and the Jao Mae Tub Tim Shrine

East Rooftop Bar at G Hua Hin Resort

The only bar with a view! East Rooftop bar has the swankiest vibes in Hua Hin along with top-notch cocktails. This is the place to go if you want to drink something more sophisticated than a Gin & Tonic. Music is always going - a mix between DJs and live bands! Rock up solo and take a seat at the bar. You'll be chatting with international strangers in no time.

Open: Daily 5:00pm – 2:00am
Where: Central Beachfront / G Hua Hin Resort & Mall

(Use this page to take notes!)

Highlights & Activities

Hua Hin Waterpark

It's hot. Why not? Vana Nava Hua Hin Water Jungle is the real deal with thrilling water slides and raft rides that spin you in circles while hurling you over dizzying courses! The main attraction is the Freefall Slide where you stand on a trap door 18 meters above ground and when it's released, you plummet through the slide at 31 miles per house. There is also an adventure park with rock walls, zip lines and a ropes course.

Pro Tip

Check online for Vana Nava's Seafood and Free – Flow Beer Promotions that start at 500 baht. Seafood at a waterpark? It's Thailand! Yes!

Open: Daily 10:00am – 6:00pm
How Much: $36 USD / 1200 baht
Where: 129/99 Soi Moo Baan Nong Kae

Wat Huay Mongkol Temple

Just 9 miles south of the village of Tub Tai, you can find the largest statue of Luang Phor Thuad, one of Thailand's most revered monks. It stands at roughly 12 meters high and 10 meters wide. Luang Phor Thuad is known for his miracles, and many Thai people go here year-round to ask for luck, health, and fortune. His most popular miracle was turning saltwater into drinkable water. It's also believed that amulets in his image give protection and safety from natural disasters and accidents. You can get these amulets in the shops nearby!

Open: 8am – sunset
Where: 30 minutes inland from the Hua Hin Market

KBA-Kiteboarding Asia

Hua Hin gets the best wind in Thailand, attracting kiteboarders from all over Asia. No matter your skill level, you too can catch some air. With one of Asia's best kiteboarding schools right here in Hua Hin, first timers can learn the ropes and novice kite boarders can improve their skills. The instructors at KBA-Kiteboarding Asia are certified by the International Kiteboarding Organization and come from all over the world – they definitely speak your language. You can take a 1-day basic flying course to give you a feel for the sport or commit to a 3-day course, which has more info on body dragging and technique.

Starting at: $120 USD / 4000 baht
Where: 143/8 Soi 75/1, Prachuap Khiri Khan,
Contact: KiteBoardingAsia.com

"Feast Thailand" - Hua Hin's #1 Food Tour

Get a taste of all of Thailand's local cuisine in one go by signing up for the Feast Thailand food tour! They have a lot of different kinds of half-day tours ranging from 1350 to 1850 baht per head. The 'Eat Like a Local' is their most popular foodie tour, which includes 15 tastings from the locals' favorite vendors! There is also a "4 Corners of Thailand" tour that introduces you to flavors from each region of the country. Depending on the tour, your food adventure will usually last around 2 to 3 hours with a fun and fabulous English-speaking guide.

Starting at: $41 USD / 1350 baht
Facebook Contact: Feast Thailand

Markets & Nightlife

In Hua Hin – markets and nightlife are one in the same. Here are the best night markets to explore – and while you're shopping, you'll run into hole in the wall bars and live music. Go with the flow, babe.

Soi Bintabat Walking Street

If bar hopping is the goal, then Soi Bintabaht is your destination! Good music, cheap drinks, and pool games! If you want to check out the local bands, El Murphy's regularly has live music and the best Mexican food.
Open: Every night

Cicada Night Market

Packed with handicrafts, trinkets, and other goods, the Cicada Night Market is the go-to place for local artists to parade their stuff! From self-portrait paintings to small glass-blown figurines, you'll find unique and artistic souvenirs that reflect modern Thai art. And of course, there is street food galore!

Open: Friday-Sunday from 4pm to 11pm.

Hua Hin Night Market

This night market checks all the boxes for what you'd expect at a typical Thai night market, plus something really unique: The Crayfish Market. Hua Hin is popular for their crayfish, lobsters and langoustines (looks like a mix between a shrimp and a lobster). Freshly caught and sitting on ice or even still alive, you can pick your dinner and watch it prepared right in front of you!
When: 6pm
Where: Hua Hin center – just head towards the railway line

How to Get Around Hua Hin

By Foot

Hua Hin is a small town which means that the major tourist spots are usually within walking distances from your accommodation.

Bicycle

Not much of a walker? Bikes are available to rent at 1.50 USD / 30 baht per hour.

Songthaew

There are four major routes that this public transport traverses. You can hop on and hop off, each ride costing you about 10 baht. Gaps in between songthaews vary from 10 to 30 minutes between 6 AM to 6 PM. During peak season, they may be available until 9 PM but at a higher cost the later it gets.

Samlor

Samlors are like rickshaws and contribute to Hua Hin's small-town charm. Pay around 2 USD / 40 baht per ride.

Getting There / Getting into Town

 From Bangkok

Option 1: By Minivan
Head to the Southern Bus Terminal!

How Much: Up to 6 USD / 200 baht
How Long: 3 hours
When: 4 AM to 12 MN

Option 2: By Airport Bus
You can take a bus straight from Bangkok Suvarnabhumi Airport.

How Much: Up to 8 USD / 260 baht
How Long: 3 hours
When: Every 1.5 hours

Option 2: By Train
You can take any of the trains headed south, passing through Hua Hin.

How Much: Starting at 90 baht
How Long: 4 hours
When: I recommend taking the express train from Hua Lumphong Station leaving at 7:45 AM.

Section 3:

The Lower Gulf of Thailand

Region #2

The Lower Gulf of Thailand

 Easy Term: The East Coast Islands

 Includes:
- ✓ Koh Samui
- ✓ Koh Phangan
- ✓ Koh Tao
- ✓ Ang Thong National Marine Park

 Best for...
- Infinity pools, social beaches, boat trips

 Known for...
- The Full Moon Party & amazing resorts

 Best time to Visit: February - July

Chapter 9: Koh Samui

You know those blacklight mosquito traps that you turn on at night? They are so bright that they attract all of the mosquitos to one small area and leave the rest of the space totally mosquito-free. Koh Samui is kind of like that – but the blacklight lamp is actually a beach club or night market.

Have I lost you yet?

The beauty of Koh Samui is this:

Half of the island is totally developed with infinity pool resorts and live music venues – attracting the tourists and travelers.

The other half of the island is unspoiled and well-preserved with waterfalls, gorgeous beaches and prime snorkeling spots.

This island really is the best of both worlds and the perfect one-stop-shop for the solo girl who is working with a tight schedule.

Koh Samui is relatively easy to get to and once you're there- you can stay put while soaking up all the Thai culture, beaches, and activities you can handle. As an almost perfect circular island with a road wrapping all the way around, you can beach hop all day long.

Are you in love yet?
You will be after this chapter…

Island Breakdown

On this island, each beach has their own personality and sets the tone for the kind of vacation you'll create for yourself.

Bophut Beach

Coco Tam's

Also known as Fisherman's Village, Bophut has a boutique feel to it where everything just feels personal! Stay here for a week and people will start to recognize your face. As for the beach, I call it "Body Scrub Beach," in that the sand is grainy but soft. The water is perfect for a shallow dip and a DIY scrub.

Mae Nam

For the girl who came here for the beaches, head to the quite coast of Mae Nam. The sand is powdery and white. The water is turquoise and warm. Staying in Mae Nam is perfect for luxury resorts and quiet guesthouses!

Silent Beach

Also known as Ban Tai Beach, this place feels like Samui's best kept secret. Down a long jungle road is this peaceful and pristine white beach that shares its shores with the ultra-fancy W Hotel and a few other lazy beach bars.

Chaweng Beach

The most western area and home to the best nightlife on Koh Samui, Chaweng Beach is a great place to set up camp. Bars, restaurants, hotels, shopping – it's all here.

Lamai Beach

Lamai is the 2nd most popular vacation beach, situated just below Chaweng. The sand is soft, the water is great for swimming, and the energy is a bit toned down compared to Chaweng, while still offering options in terms of hotels and nightlife.

Lipa Noi Beach

The central west coast beach, Lipa Noi offers the best sunset views! Lipa Noi has a more "beach town" feel with a collection of bars and restaurants with chilled out vibes, yet plenty of options when it comes to food and budget.

Accommodation in Koh Samui

Maenam

Sensimar Resort and Spa – Adults Only 16+

My #1 pick for a luxury resort on Koh Samui – Sensimar Resort and Spa will throw you into full-on vacation mode the second you arrive. Suites overlook the glittering pool and ocean with pillow-soft beds and private balconies, but girl, the private pool rooms are a game changer. Stay in a private pool villa where you can turn the music up and tan topless with a pool that is big enough to do laps. When you're ready to put your top back on, head to the pool.

The eccentric infinity pool is truly an art piece. There are over 20 sunbeds with poolside service and the same goes for the beachfront sunbeds – the staff will bring that margarita to you! When you're not sunning, mingle with other guests at the swim up pool bar – happy hour starts at 4pm with 2 for 1 cocktails. The beach is only a few steps away with powdery soft sand and free kayaks to get your heart pumping.

Speaking of, Sensimar offers daily workout classes for guests including sunrise yoga and private training sessions in the gym – free of charge.

The restaurant is full service with steak and pasta cooked to perfection and a wine list that is perfect for pairing. Try the Caprese Salad... I couldn't get enough. Truly an experience worth every penny. Treat yourself, babe.

Style: Privates
Starts at: $110 USD / 3700 baht
Where: Maenam Beach
Address: 44/134 Moo 1, Maenam Beach

Treehouse Silent Beach Resort

One of Mae Nam's best kept secrets, Treehouse Silent Beach Resort is pure zen. Silent Beach has white sand and clean water for swimming. The bungalows range from backpacker-budget huts to mid-range sea view villas with air-conditioning. The restaurant is my favorite on the island – known for healthy food made with clean ingredients. Try the Mojitos – they come in every flavor. The bar lights up with tiki torches at night. Have a drink here and then walk down to the swanky W Hotel and pretend to be fancy in their beachfront palace bar.

Heads Up: Intimate and exclusive, sometimes you can only book through their website - tree-house.org

Style: Privates
Starts at: $10 - $45 USD / 300 – 1500 baht
Where: Bophut Beach
Address: 12/2 Moo 1 Soi Rainbow Maenam

Khwan Beach Resort – Luxury Glamping and Pool Villas Samui - Adults Only

Have you died and gone to glamping heaven? Quite possibly, yes. Khwan Beach Resort is the most surreal hotel stay you'll have this entire trip. The pool is bright and spacious with a massive waterfall and inviting swim-up bar. The glamping tents don't feel like tents...but don't feel like villas either. They have princess style beds, lavish bathtubs and even a backyard. Equipped with air-conditioning, they are comfortable in dry season. And because they're tents, they are exciting to sleep in during rainy season.

Style: Privates
Starts at: $97 USD/ 3200 baht
Where: 5-minute walk to Maenam Beach
Address: 67/61 Moo 1, Maenam

Bophut & Fisherman's Village

The Waterfront Boutique Hotel

The best and most affordable resort in Fisherman's Village! The Waterfront is located at the very end of walking street – which means no noise but instant access to all the best shopping and restaurants. It's also located at the very end of Bophut Beach – which means peace, privacy, and the cleanest water. Flop on a lounge chair in the sand and run into the sea when you get too hot. Back in the bungalows, you've got a fabulous rain shower and one of the comfiest beds I've ever slept in. Breakfast in the morning is cooked to order and the British owner, Robin, is around to give you local tips…or just shoot the shit.

Style: Privates
Starts at: $60 USD/ 2000 baht
Where: Bo Phut Beach
Address: 71/2 M. 1, Bo Phut, Koh Samui

Riviera Hotel

Get the sea view room. I guarantee that you won't make it 24 hours without looking out and saying "Oh my god" at least once. This tiny 3-story guest house makes you feel like you are waking up IN the ocean. The beds are huge, there are English channels on TV and the balcony is everything!!! To get your tan on, go downstairs and drag a

bean bag to the sand. Flop down and people watch until you're ready
to go explore Fisherman's Village.

Style: Privates
Starts at: $50 USD / 1700 baht
Where: Bophut Beach
Address: 6/1 M.1, Bophut, Fisherman's Village

Chaweng Beach

Liquid Lounge Hostel $

A party hostel with dignity! Liquid Lounge has managed to do the
impossible. They've created a hostel that is clean, comfortable and
respectable, while merging a social bar that feels playful and inclusive
to every guest regardless of age or background. Join the daily happy
hour in the lounge that is designed to naturally connect you with
other guests – you don't have to put in much effort to meet people
here. Drink some beers, play some games, and then go explore
Chaweng together. When you come back, some seriously comfy beds
will be waiting to absorb your hangover.

Heads Up: Be diligent on choosing an accurate check-in time or
keeping the hostel updated if you're going to be late.

Style: Privates
Starts at: $9 USD/ 500 baht
Where: Chaweng Beach
Address: 11/3 Moo 2, Chaweng Beach Road, Bophut

Cheeky Monkey Samui Hostel $

Be comfortable on a budget with this rooftop pool, happy-hour
hangout hostel that feels more like a hotel than a backpacker's spot.
You get a private room that is immaculately clean with reception that
is more than willing to help book boats and buses for you. Make
some friends and walk 15 minutes to the center of town for some
nighttime exploring. Then come back to your quiet room away from
the chaos.

Style: Privates
Starts at: $15 USD/ 500 baht
Where: Chaweng Beach
Address: 6/14 M.3 , Beach Rd, Bophut

Lub d Hostel and Beachfront Resort $

Lub d Koh Samui is the newest edition to the glamourous Lub d hostel network. Feeling more like a social resort than a hostel, you'll find that everything here is just a little bit...extra. From the beachfront catamaran hammocks to the Floating DJ booth, swim up bar and infinity pool... there's no reason to stay anywhere else if tropical vibes are what you're after. Lub d Samui offers accommodation to suit all styles, from the thriftiest of backpackers to the fanciest Flashpackers (backpackers with a bigger budget)! Pack your cutest suits. Vacation starts here.

Ps. Lub d translates to "sleep well" in Thai, and here on Koh Samui - it's no different. Sleep safe, sleep well, and if you're going to miss sleep, they'll give you a party worth missing sleep for.

Style: Dorms & Privates
Starts at: $15 - $80 USD / 500 – 2,650 baht
Where: Chaweng Beach

Montien House $$

Instead of staying at the coveted beach club, Ark Bar, stay right next door. You can remain within walking distance to the action but get some actual sleep without techno music blaring in your dreams. Montien House is sandwiched between the best of Chaweng with the best shopping and restaurants on one end, and the beach on the other. The pool villas here are amazing and affordable – by the way! They are spacious, clean, and a fun place to bring a boy (just sayin').

Style: Privates

Starts at: $50 USD / 1700 baht
Where: Chaweng Beach
Address: 5 Moo 2, Bophut, Koh Samui

Malibu Koh Samui Resort & Beach Club $$$

I have a relay race for you to complete: ready and go! Check in to your garden villa surrounded by tall trees and fresh air. Then throw on your suit and head to the pool overlooking the ocean. Do at lap to the end and hop onto the sand. Take a dip in the warm water and then collapse onto a bean bag on the beach. Order a hand tossed pizza and devour it by candlelight with your toes in the sand. Feeling accomplished?

Style: Privates
Starts at: $75 USD/ 2500 baht
Where: Chaweng Beach

Baan Talay Resort $$$

Vacay like a celebrity at this glamorous island resort! Located just south of the center of Chaweng Beach, Baan Talay Resort offers the perfect balance between peaceful and party. Spend you day soaking up the sun and then stroll into town at night for some shopping and people watching. The location is amazing, the staff treat you like royalty, and the attention to detail here makes this place feel 5-star.

Style: Privates
Starts at: $118 USD/ 4,000 baht
Where: Chaweng Beach

The Library $$$$

When a resort has a "pillow menu," you know it's going to be fancy. Famous for its bright red infinity pool overlooking the water and futuristic architecture, The Library is a splurge that's worth it just for the photos alone! Rooms range from "Smart Studios" with 42-inch plasma TVs with all the good channels to "Secret Pool Villas" that are just over the top. You must try The Drink Gallery and The Tapas Bar where they're just as creative with cocktails and dishes.

Style: Privates
Starts at: $342 USD / 11,300 baht
Where: Chaweng Beach
Address: 14/1 Moo.2 Chaweng Beach, Bo Phut, Koh Samui

Lamai Beach

Tiki Tiki Beach Hostel $

Spend money like a backpacker, vacation like a trust-fund baby.
Inside, your dorm room is basic with beds that are just fine and
shared bathrooms. Put on your sexiest swimsuit and step out into the
beach front pool and bar that will make you feel like you're actually
paying 4x the price. With tree swings hanging from shady branches
and white sand between your toes – this place is the definition of a
steal. Plus, the hostel is quite intimate which makes meeting people
and making friends a breeze!

Style: Dorms
Starts at: $10 USD/ 300 baht
Where: Lamai Beach
Address: 441/14 Tambon Maret Main road, Ampheu Koh Samui

Am Samui Palace $$

Ya know what makes for the perfect resort pool? Multiple surfaces to
lay and tan, along with a swim-up pool bar where you can meet the
potential love of your life…or some friendly Germans. Check and
check. Am Samui Palace has a spacious pool and spacious rooms to
match. Go for the pool access rooms where you can slip into the
water from your room or stalk your pretty from the veranda.

Style: Privates
Starts at: $50 USD/ 1700 baht
Where: Lamai Beach
Address: 124/39 Moo3, T.Maret

The Privilege Hotel Ezra Royal Beach $$

If private pools are what you're after, come check out this bargain.
The Privilege Hotel Ezra Resort has some of the most gorgeous villas
and private pools on the island for ½ the price of Chaweng, and in
my opinion – has a much better location. You are far removed from
the party but still on a serene beach with plenty of beach bars and
restaurants to choose from.

Style: Privates
Starts at: $73 USD/ 2330 baht
Where: Lamai Beach
Address: 156/1 Moo 4. Lamai Beach T-Maret

Off the Beaten Path

Aforetime Beach House $

If you don't have time to hop over to Koh Phangan or Koh Tao, but still want to experience what small island living is like – here is a pretty great representation. Snuggle into an intimate hostel with hosts that take such pride in hospitality. Everything here feels personal with Joe and Champoo taking you under their wing. You'll find likeminded travelers at this hostel – people who want to explore local night markets and take a kayak around the bay. Real connections are made here.

Style: Dorms
Starts at: $9 USD/ 270 baht
Where: Lipa Noi Beach

Sea Valley Hotel & Spa $$

A picturesque resort nestled under palm trees next to the ocean – totally off the beaten path and away from the tourist scene on Koh Samui – Sea Valley is a must. Hours melt away easily at this resort. After a fabulous breakfast, float between the pool, the beach, and the free kayaks that glide over this especially calm bay. End the day with some pampering spa services to nourish your newly sun-kissed skin.

Style: Privates
Starts at: $57 USD/ 1890 baht
Where: Lipa Noi Beach

Samui Caravans $$

A caravan + camping community on the beach – come join this quirky family! You can sleep super cheap in a beachfront tent or splurge for the experience of sleeping in a camper van equipped with a toilet and flat screen TV. The property is literally spitting distance from one of the most gorgeous white sand beaches you've ever seen. And it gets better. Kayaking, snorkeling and real coffee are free. You are within 5 to 10-minute walking distance of bars and restaurants in either direction. The hosts become instant friends and will show you the ropes and help you climb em'. Come stay for one night…and I bet you'll end up booking two.

Style: Tents and Caravans
Starts at: $3 - $91 USD/ 90 - 3000 baht
Where: Laem Sor Beach

Where to Eat on Samui

So many night markets! If you're planning dinner, check the night market schedule first.

The Black Pearl

It's always a good sign when you see both Thai and Western people eating in a restaurant! I was introduced to this secret spot by a local Thai girl. Sitting at the very end of Lamai Beach, the sand is powdery soft and the rock formations in the water make for a great view while you eat. Order the whole grilled fish (Nam Pla) and Green Papaya Sala (Som Tam) – just let them know how spicy you like it. They've got lots of fresh squid, shrimp and veggie plates, too – and for super reasonable prices.

Open: Daily 8:00 am – 10:30 pm
Where: Lamai
Address: 127/64 Moo 3, Maret

The Jungle Club

The views are insane at the Jungle Club. This should be one of the first restaurants or pitstops on your trip in Samui. The Jungle Club really sets the tone for the rest of your trip. Melt into a bean bag chair and order off one of the best Thai and western tapas menus on the island. Drinks can be a bit pricey but consider it a premium for the view!

Where: Bophut
Address: Soi Panyadee, Bophut, Ko Samui

Silent Beach Resort

The most popular dish on the menu is one you've got to try: Khao Soi. This northern noodle soup is served with juicy chicken in a fragrant coconut milk broth and topped with crispy wonton noodles. It's a staple in Thai culture, but a dish that isn't very well-known in the west. Now is your chance to try something you may never find at Thai restaurants back home.

Aside from Khao Soi, Silent Beach Resort is known for their healthy, yet totally yummy menu options like hummus, falafel wraps, Indian dahl and all things vegetarian. Plus, every day there is a 4pm to 7pm Mojito Happy Hour with 99-baht tropical mojitos of every kind!

Ps. This is a super local & expat spot – not too many tourists know about this place. I find that kind of fun...

Where: Mae Nam
Address: 12/2 Moo 1 Soi Rainbow Maenam
Open: Lunch to 10pm

The Hut – Thai Food

A Thai restaurant that is jam-packed every night...even in low season! That's a damn good sign. The Hut's ambiance is simple and relaxed, run by a Thai family who hurries each dish out piping hot. They specialize in traditional curries and tempura everything! Nothing fancy, just classic food with fresh ingredients.

Where: Fisherman's Village, across from The Waterfront Boutique
Address: 3/3 Moo 1 Fisherman's Village, Bophut
Open: Daily 1pm – 10pm / In low season, open just for dinner

RockPool Samui Restaurant

Uninterrupted jaw-dropping views of the ocean, Rockpool Restaurant is a hidden gem that you must visit while you're here! Bring your appetite and your flip flops to this waterfront restaurant with a little sandy beach below. I love this place for tapas like calamari and oysters on the half shell. They've also got fantastic wood fired pizza! Come for lunch and a dip in the beach below, or venture over for Happy Hour, every day from 5-7pm for two-for- one drinks.

Open: Daily 7am-10pm
Where: Bophut
Address: 80/32 Moo 5, Kanda Residences Samui

Roman Restaurant and Bar

At Roman, you'll find Turkish food using a blend of local and imported ingredients to create mouthwatering dishes! Dine on some hummus with fresh pita bread or a Turkish pizza while you sip a generous glass of wine and mellow out to the tunes of live music.

Where: Mae Nam
Address: 215/6 Moo 1, Mae Nam, Ko Samui
Open: Daily 6pm – 10pm

The Shack

The place to go for steak and wine! The Shack imports all of their juicy cuts of meat from lamb shanks and ribs to the juiciest steaks – even compared to the steaks you've been eating back home! And since you're on vacation in Thailand, treat yourself to a true Surf and Turf with local lobster and Tiger prawns.

Pro Tip

When you sit down, tell your server that "The Waterfront Resort" sent you and you *should* get 20% off your bill.

Where: Bo Phut
Address: 88/3 Moo 1 Fisherman's Village, Bophut
Open: Daily 5:30pm – 10:30pm

Green Bird – Thai Food

It's safe to say that Green Bird is the most famous Thai Food restaurant in Chaweng. Their colorful menu includes all of the Thai staples you love, and also introduces you to a variety of classic Thai dishes that you certainly wouldn't find at home. Order the Razor Clams with Basil, the mussels with spicy Thai dipping sauce, or the Pad Thai wrapped in Omelette. Finish it all off with Mango Sticky Rice and now, you've officially conquered true Thai food!

Open: Daily 11:00 am – 10:00 pm
Where: Chaweng
Address: 157/17 Moo 2 Chaweng Beach Road

No Stress

It's impossible to be anything but totally euphoric at this beachfront bistro – hence the name. Take a break from the sun and pop in for a fresh and nutritious lunch with an ocean view. Massive burgers, seafood BBQ, and the must-try Scandinavian Mussels are enough to put you into a full-on food coma. But don't worry, they have lounge chairs on the beach perfect for a quick nap.

Where: Lamai Beach
Open: Daily 8:30am – 6pm

The Islander Pub & Restaurant

Amazing nachos. Juicy burgers. Thick steak. How does that sound? Add some classic cocktails and cheap beers and you've got it made at The Islander. Sports fans, they've got games going on big screens around the bar. If you've got a particular game coming up, let the manager know.

Where: Central Chaweng Beach
Open: Noon to Midnight

Poppies Samui

If you happen to visit Koh Samui on a holiday like Christmas or Thanksgiving, check out Poppie's Holiday Menu. They put on special feasts for special occasions. Every other day of the year, they serve both Thai and international dishes in a charming tropical garden setting with a full view of the ocean. AND every Saturday night, they put on a traditional Thai dance performance. Get a little fancy.

Where: South Chaweng Beach − right before Samui Lagoon Bay
Open: Daily 11:30am - 10:30pm

Feel Travel Samui Thai Restaurant

Authentic Thai food made for a western palate means not too spicy and nothing too crazy! Travel is a popular spot for Thai Food beginners. Start with something you know, like Pad Thai and Spring Rolls, and add in something you don't know, like Penang Curry or Pad See Ew noodles. If there was ever a time to safely step outside your food comfort zone, this is it. Ingredients are fresh, flavors are balanced, and the staff speak enough English to understand your preferences.

Where: O K Village
Open: Daily 6pm − 10pm

Highlights & Activities

Big Buddha Temple

Wat Phra Yai is the most popular Buddhist Temple on Koh Samui and for good reason, starting with its impressive size. 12-meters high and covered in reflective gold paint, Wat Phra Yai shimmers under the sun which you can see from the bottom of the 45-step staircase leading up to the giant statue. Sitting in the classic mediation pose known as "Buddha defying Mara" – or resisting temptation to reach enlightenment.

Before you head up the stairs, visit the monk sitting to the left under the shade. You can give a donation of 20 baht, and then kneel with your hands in prayer and head down, as he blesses you with incense and holy water.

Head up the stairs- just take your shoes off first- and walk around the temple as you ring each prayer bell for good luck. Want to make your dreams come true? Before you go, take a 10-baht coin, make a wish and throw it up onto Buddha's lap. If the coin stays, your wish will come true.

Where: Bophut
Address: Route 4171, Bophut, Ko Samui

Wat Plai Laem

In my opinion, this is the most impressive temple grounds on Koh Samui, but half as many tourists visit here!

What makes this temple so special is that it combines Buddhism and Hinduism. There are countless statutes and temples that pay tribute to the gods, spirits, and ancestors – you can easily spend 30 minutes walking around in awe.

But the most awe-inspiring of all is Wat Plai Laem, the 18-arm statue of Guanyin, the Goddess of Mercy and Compassion. Colorful, unique, and #FemaleEmpowerment, Guanyin is believed to be a source of unconditional love, a protector of all beings and a fertility goddess. She is the Goddess to whom local women come to pray for a child, and healthy family.

Before you go, walk towards the small shop in the center of the compound and you'll see a fish food machine. Drop in a coin, take a basket and collect your fish food that looks more like cat food. Go to the lake and start feeding the fish – you'll be shocked by all the creatures that rise up from the depths.

Go to the fresh market next to Thong Sala Pier and buy a live turtle for about 150 baht. The lady will bag it…just make sure he can breathe! When you get to the temple, you'll cross a small bridge leading to Wat Plai Laem Temple. In this pond, you release your turtle and the god bring you good karma and luck for your deed.

Where: Bo Phut – 1.9 miles east of Wat Phra Yai
Address: Wat Plai Laem, Road 4171

Grandma and Grandpa Rock

Can you spot Grandma and Grandpa? In Lamai, there is a gorgeous rocky peninsula that jets into the water giving you gorgeous views of Lamai beach and the bay. There's more to do here than just enjoy the view, however. There are two rocks that represent Grandma and Grandpa. Grandpa is pretty easy to find, Grandma take a bit of effort, don't be afraid to ask someone where to find her. Once you see them, congratulations, you officially understand Thai humor in a nutshell. Oh, and there are some cute boutiques and a little street market on the way down to the rocks!

Where: Lamai
Address: 92 84310 126/92 Moo 3 Ko Samui District

Go Snorkeling

There are two ways to get your face in the water!

Option 1: By Beach
Rent a mask for the day and beach hop by motorbike. You're after the beaches with the most preserved coral and thus, the best underwater marine life.

- ✓ Coral Cove
- ✓ Taling Ngam
- ✓ Ao Phang Ka
- ✓ Tongsai Bay Resort
- ✓ Crystal Bay Resort

Option 2: By Boat
Go into any tour office and ask about a snorkel boat trip! You can be on a boat within hours that will take you to some gorgeous islands and middle-of-nowhere reef spots.

You can also join a bigger island-hopping tour like the Angthong Marine Park Day Tour that includes snorkeling but isn't all about snorkeling.

And for perhaps the best – but more expensive – snorkel trips, go into a dive shop! Dive shop snorkel trips are less crowded and more fun as the crew speak English and like to avoid the masses.

Watch a Muay Thai Fight

Brad Weeks Photography

When you're walking down the streets of Chaweng, you'll see and hear trucks driving through the center blasting advertising for 'big Muay Thai fight tonight!' There's always a fight going on at Chaweng Boxing Stadium, often featuring western fighters which is a pretty thrilling sight to see.

Pro Tip

Free Muay Thai Match in Lamai on Saturday Nights from evening to 10pm. You're expected to buy a drink when you're in there – but they won't force you if you say, "Later later".

Where: Chaweng Boxing Stadium
Cost: Around 1500 baht

Want to try your hands at a Muay Thai Boxing Class? Try Jackie Muay Thai – 1st lesson is 400 baht

Ride a Motorbike Around the Island

If – and only if - you are an experienced motorbike driver…continue reading. The roads on Koh Samui can be chaotic, but if you're comfortable on a bike and can navigate a road with truck drivers and cars - the loop around Koh Samui is pretty fun. Use your GPS, and wear one headphones with one earphone to listen to directions and leave one ear free to listen to traffic. GPS has mapped everything from waterfalls, restaurants, beaches and temples. The west coast of the island is much less chaotic than driving on the east coast, by the way.

Have a Bikini Day

Nikki Beach Club and Ark Bar are the two most popular beach clubs! Drink specials, lounge chairs, DJs and the ultimate place to socialize with people from all over the world!

Ark Bar is on Chaweng Beach.
Nikki Beach Club is on Lipa Noi.

Ark Bar is more convenient and crowded.
Nikki Beach Club is the place for amazing sushi and cocktails.
*Write to Nikki Beach Club and see if they'll do a free hotel pick-up, something that they offer in the low-seasons or on slow-days.

The Best Tours

As with nearly every popular tour in Thailand, all of these tours are easy to join! Go into any tour office and buy a ticket. These tour offices sell tickets for the same 5 or 6 companies that offer identical tours. The only thing that differs from day to day is the weather and the people you get lucky enough to be paired with for the day!

Here are the tours that are worth your time!

Ang Thong Marine Park Day Tour

Ang Thong Marine Park is one of the most stunning underwater habitats in the Gulf of Thailand. There are 42 islands total, all with preserved corals and protected marine life. And you can see them up close with this incredible tour.

Wake up bright and early - a car will be at your hotel waiting to pick you up at 7:30 am. Next stop, the pier! You'll board a speed boat with about 30 other tourists from all over the world. You'll put on life jackets and be given a quick brief on the day. Then you'll be handed your snorkel and the fun begins.

- ✓ Island Viewpoints to see the whole Marine Park
- ✓ Small deserted white sand beaches and islands
- ✓ Snorkeling with colorful schools of fish, eels, and urchins
- ✓ Local Thai food lunch and cold bottles of water.

The whole day is a whirlwind of tropical paradise!

How Much: Average $54 USD / 1800 baht

Samui Quad Bike Tour

Take your pick between a 1 or 2-hour quad bike tour through the jungles of Koh Samui. As you follow your guide over red dirt roads and small river streams, you'll pass stunning viewpoints of the ocean and island shore below. When you take the two-hour tour, you drive out to a remote waterfall in the jungle and go for a swim in the cool, clear pool below, followed by a drink at this secluded bar in the jungle.

How Much: $54 USD / 1800 baht
How Long: 1 hour
Contact: SamuiQuadATV.com

Markets & Shopping

Monday: Mini Fisherman's Village Walking Street
Thursday: Mae Nam Night Market
Friday: Fisherman's Village Walking Street
Sunday: Lamai Night Market
Daily: Chaweng Night Market, Chaweng Walking Street, Lamai Night Plaza

Lamai Sunday Night Market

Come hungry and leave full. This market offers everything from BBQ chicken to Japanese-Thai Fusion. There's also a ton of food here, including fried everything! They've got friend chicken, fried shrimp, and my favorite…fried bugs! With a kebab in one hand and a Thai Tea in the other, you can watch crazy antics like Muay Thai street fights or shop the knock-off makeup section!

Where: Lamai Beach
Open: Sunday 4:30pm-Midnight

Fisherman's Village Walking Street

Popular for their gourmet street food, Fisherman's Village Walking Street is One of the biggest and best night markets in Koh Samui, held every Friday. This night market just keeps going and going, following one long walking street. You can't leave without some souvenirs! Get your bargaining pants on and get ready to haggle for colorful handbags, surprisingly high-quality swim suits and elephant pants of every color. You can find t-shirts for 100 baht and jewelry for even cheaper.

Open: Monday and Friday 5pm-11pm
Where: Bophut Beach Road

Mae Nam Night Market

One of the less crowded night markets in terms of tourists, Mae Nam gives you VIP access to all the best night market elements. Fresh food, wooden handicrafts, cotton tops and "almost genuine" RayBans are the highlights here. Keep walking towards the end of the road and you'll come across a charming Chinese temple that's work a look.

Open: Thursday 5:00pm - midnight
Where: Mae Nam Center

Central Festival Mall

Last but not least, Central Festival Mall! Right next to Hooters, you'll find this western-style mall with Uniqlo, Nike, Adidas and some western brands that moved to Thailand to die...like Playboy and RipCurl. The main attraction here, for me at least, is Tops Market. This grocery store has everything you could ever want: fresh fruit, fresh sushi being prepared in front of you, imported craft beer, cheap beer, snacks, cheese – you name it.

Open: 11:00am – 11:00pm
Address: 209/3 MOO 2, Bophut, Koh Samui, Surat Thani, 8432

Chaweng Walking Street

As you meander through the stalls with a coconut in your hand, you're surrounded by live music and the hustling of vendors trying to strike a deal with potential customers. Shopping on Chaweng Walking Street is abundant!

Famously known for its fresh seafood, which you can see swimming around in fish tanks, you'll also want to save room for a bite to eat.

You can pick up anything here from grilled chicken to sticky rice, as well as smoothies and cold beer right out of the cooler.

The market is one of the biggest in Koh Samui and just a stone's throw away from the largest and most popular beach on the east side of the island, Chaweng Beach. It's a must-visit while you're here.

Pro Tip

When haggling for a bargain on a stall always smile at the owner and joke around with them to secure the best price. Walk away when the price is too steep, and it might magically drop.

Open: 4:30pm – 12am (no shopping stalls on Fridays and Sundays)
Where: South of Chaweng's main drag
Address: The walking street begins near La Fortune Restaurant

Chaweng Night Market

More of a big food court than a shopping area, Thais and travelers alike can be found perched atop a bar side stool drinking 100 baht beers and 250 baht buckets. Chaweng is lined with these little stalls where meeting new people is easy.

Open: 5pm-11pm
Where: Chaweng Beach Road – behind Star Gym
Address: 14/102 Moo 2

Koh Samui Nightlife

Ark Bar

Sitting on 150 meters of beach front property, Ark Bar has made the loud and clear statement that they are party central on Chaweng Beach! During the day, join the pool party with a swim up bar. At night, party goers are lured in with live DJs and fire spinners. The vibes here stay pretty mellow with tropical cocktails and beachfront lounge chairs- but the fun doesn't stop until at least 2am.

Where: Chaweng Beach
Open: Daily 7am-2am

Chaweng Center

Bar hopping is the thing to do in Chaweng. Like a school of fish, people seem to flow together or follow the live music. There are hole in the wall bars, music venues with amazing cover bands and a couple sleazy bars where you can catch a glimpse of the old man – Thai girl relationships.
The most popular bars to visit on any given night:
- The Palm
- Green Mango
- Hendrix

- Stadium
- Henry Afrika

Hush Bar Samui

In the mood to dance and mingle? Throw yourself onto the dance floor at Hush Bar – where every night there is a different DJ spinning everything from Hip Hop & RnB to UK Garage, Commercial House, Dubstep and Drum n Bass. They've got super cheap buckets until 9pm, just remember to watch your drink and take it easy! Hush Bar's reputation is just fine – just keep your wits about you, my love.

Heads Up: After Hush Bar, the crowd usually flows to the next dance/clubbing spot – Stadium which is open til 7am.

Where: Soi Green Mango, Chaweng Beach
Open: Daily 7pm-2:30am

On Street Bar

Not the house-music clubbing type of gal? No problem. On Street Bar is a quirky little watering hole next to KC Beach Club- so tiny that you might miss it if you're not paying attention. Built with upcycled tin walls and decorated with a collection of colorful light fixtures and random figurines- consider this the speak easy of Koh Samui. Live music, cheap beer, good people.

Where: Chaweng Road next to KC Beach Club
Open: Daily 7pm-2am+

Starz Cabaret

No matter how hard us girls try, we will never be as feminine or glamourous as a lady boy – and this show proves it. At a glance, you'd never know these glamourous stage performers covered in feathers and pearls were born as boys. They are so sensual and feminine as they glide across the stage, performing choreographed dance numbers and over-the-top lip-syncing Britney Spears bits. Each show is 45 minutes long and your entrance includes one drink.

How much: $7 USD / 220 baht
When: 3 shows daily – 8:30pm, 9:30pm & 10:30pm
Where: Chaweng - 1st floor at Khun Chaweng Resort
Address: 200/11 Moo 2, Chaweng Beach Road

CocoTam's

A must-visit, no matter where you're staying on the island. Get you cute butt up to CocoTam's for cocktails on the beach. This sprawling beachfront bar feels like an adult playground: There are bar-side swings for chairs, catamaran style net beds, bean bags in the sand, movies every night, two pool tables, and a beer pong table. YET, they keep things real classy and vibes stay super chill. Try a margarita or a Mango Mojito. You can trust that the alcohol is western quality – so go for it, babe.

Ps. Sitting on those swings all night is an easy way to get chatting to some new people!

Open: 1:00pm – 1:00am
Where: Bophut Fisherman's Village
Address: 62/1 moo 1 Bophut

How to Get Around Koh Samui

Grab Taxi

The Uber of Thailand. Grab Taxi is convenient because you can hook it up to your ATM card. If you run out of cash or don't want to keep track of your cash, you've got a guaranteed way to get home.

Navigo

Just like Grab Taxi and Uber, Navigo is Koh Samui's on-call driving service. I often find Navigo to be cheaper than Grab Taxi, but sometimes Grab Taxi is more convenient. It's nice to have options.

Motorbike

You can rent a motorbike on Koh Samui…but I only recommend riding during the day and avoiding driving through the busy streets of Chaweng. There is a street that loops around the whole island – it gets pretty calm on the west coast.

How to Get to Koh Samui

  From Bangkok

Fly to Surat Thani or Koh Samui

There is an international airport on Koh Samui, making flights just way to easy! I highly recommend buying a round-trip flight to Bangkok, and then buying a separate flight from Bangkok to Koh Samui.

Bangkok Airways owns the airport here and offers 14 flights per day from 6:00am to 8:30 pm. Flying time is just 1 hour!

 ### Take a Train to Surat Thani

If you're not pressed for time, the cheapest option to get to Koh Samui is to take a train from Bangkok to Surat Thani. It takes 12 hours to Surat Thani and you can catch a ferry from town.

 **From Phuket**

 ### Fly to Koh Samui

The flight is just 1 hour on a tiny propeller plane! It's so fun!

 ### Ferry Routes from Surrounding Areas

From Surat Thani

How Much: $22 USD / 720 baht
How Long: 1 hour 45 minutes
When: All day, starting at 9:00am

✦ From Koh Phangan

How Much: Starting at $5 USD / 150 baht
How Long: 30 minutes
When: All day long – last boat is usually around 7pm depending on the season

✦ From Koh Tao

How Much: $15 USD / 500 baht
How Long: 1.5 – 2.5 hours
When: All day long

Chapter 10: Koh Phangan

Koh Phangan is synonymous with parties! There's the Full Moon Party, Jungle Party, Waterfall Party and random parties every damn day of the week. While partying is certainly the main attraction on this small tropical island...there is more to Koh Phangan than just partying!

The Coast Resort

Being the fifth largest island in Thailand, Koh Phangan offers plenty of relaxing beaches and natural wonders to explore. There are day waterfalls, sand bars, viewpoints and...parties. Okay, it's a party island.

If you're coming to party, you could stay for a week and have a great time socializing and bar hopping. If you're a mild partier, 3 days on Koh Phangan is more than enough to see all there is to see!

Island Breakdown

Haad Rin Beach

Got your party pants on? Then Haad Rin Beach should be your go-to beach if you love dancing and drinking. During the day, Haad Rin Beach looks just like other beaches in Thailand. But at night, expect the entire place to light up. This place is where the Full Moon Party happens where 30,000 people gather and party the night away. Cover yourself with paint, party until morning, and drink alcohol from a bucket! This happens every full moon.

Had Wai Nam Beach

This area is characterized by crystal-clear waters, fine white sand and palm trees (surprise surprise!) There is only one hotel on Had Wai Nam Beach and just one Thai restaurant that serves both Thai and Western food. The only way to get to this beach is by a boat. There are no coral reefs here so it's ideal for swimming all year round!

Than Sadet Beach

Meaning "Royal River" in Thai, this small gorgeous beach is considered to be a sacred place. In the 18th century, several Thai kings visited this beach and even carved their initials on the enormous granite rocks.

Bottle Beach

One of my Top 10 Beaches in Thailand - Bottle Beach is stunning, unspoiled and a must-visit when on Koh Phangan. Tiny and pristine, there are only a few bungalows and restaurants tucked into the jungle, overlooking the beach.

Haad Yao Beach

One-kilometer stretch of perfect white sand makes Haad Yao Beach on of Koh Phangan's most popular spots. Within walking distance to restaurants, bars, and guest houses, staying at Haad Yao is a fabulous idea. Besides sun bathing, you can also snorkel and swim here. Total perfection!

Leela Beach

Situated opposite of Haad Rin Beach, Leela beach has the bluest waters and the softest white sand. It's one of the best swimming beaches on Koh Phangan as the waves are basically non-existent. A few resorts are available here with every budget in mind.

Chaloklum Bay

Situated north of Koh Phangan, stylish Chaloklum Bay is close to the local village where you can eat fresh fish and seafood, caught daily by the local fishermen. It's a tranquil beach perfect for travelers looking for complete relaxation. Activities you can engage in at Chaloklum Bay include windsurfing, kiting, surfing, wakeboarding, and diving.

Ban Tai Beach

The party never ends at Ban Tai Beach. During the day, it's a normal Thai beach. The sand isn't amazing, and the water is too coraly for swimming – but it's still a peaceful place to hang. Once the sun starts to set, Ban Tai transforms into party heaven. Restaurants and bars come alive with live music, drink specials and bucket drinks. Still around, it only gets wilder.

Accommodation in Koh Phangan

Lazy House Shenanigans $

Planning to party? Lazy House is the perfect location for the Full Moon Party and attracts other travelers who are into that booze bucket + fluorescent lifestyle! Plus, the hostel staff will take good care of you on a bad trip- trust me, they've seen it before. When you're not partying, hang out at the pool or chill in the common area – just be sure to book a week before the Full Moon Party…this place fills up!

Style: Dorms
Starting at: $7 USD / 220 baht
Where: Haad Rin Beach
Address: 91/13 moo 6, Haad Rin

Goodtime Backpackers $

Like to be social but also like to have your space? Goodtime Backpackers is the perfect place to mingle and relax. Start the morning off in your air-conditioned room, then migrate to the party pool or play a game of beach volleyball with the naturally social crew of travelers that migrate here. The pool is open 24/7 and so is the bar! If you're here during any big party, be it Waterfall, Jungle, or Full Moon, Goodtime Backpackers has a preparty and guests transport to the party together – creating an instant friend group. But…if humans aren't your thing, you can always just hang out with Kevin Bacon…the resident pet pig.

Style: Privates and Dorms
Starts at: $11/360 baht
Where: Less than a mile from the Centre
Address: 101/2 Moo 1 Baan Tai Road

Phangan Arena Hostel $

Imagine an adult summer camp, that's what Phangan Arena Hostel is. There's a soccer (footy) field, massive pool with bean bags all around for tanning, beer pong table, internet café, free gym, movie room, and non-stop bucket drinks- it's hard to pass this place up…especially for 100 baht dorm beds. The crowd is usually a mix of travelers in their 20's, very social, and carry on socializing well into the night. If you want to make a few friends, then get your cute butt over here.

Style: Dorms and Privates
Starting at: $15 USD / 500 baht
Where: Ban Tai
Address: 111 Moo 1 Bantai Koh Phangan

Nibbana Bungalows $$

Nibbana is your tropical dream come true. Quaint wooden bungalows facing a private beach with hammocks, lounge chairs and total peace and quiet. Wake up and do yoga with the waves. Lay down and tan in the sand. Stay up late and watch the stars in silence. Here is where you come to regroup, read, and re-center yourself. Need to pop into town? Everything is a 5-minute bike ride or a 15-minute walk…no hills!

Style: Private Bungalows
Starting at: $69 USD / 2,300 baht
Where: Private Beach
Address: 4/12 Moo 6, Hin Kong Road

Sarikantang Resort and Spa $$

On one hand, you're classy and like to spend the day sunbathing with a mojito by your side and a flower in your hair. On the other hand, you want to go to the Full Moon Party and dance your face off until the sun comes up. I feel you, girl. Sarikantang is the place to be both sophisticated and spastic. You've got this superb beachfront resort isolated on the white sands of Seekantang Beach – sunset and privacy included – which is only a 10-minute walk or free hotel tuk tuk ride to

229

Haad Rin Center where all the partying goes down. Go have a wild night and walk home to your sanctuary when you're ready.

Starting at: $54 USD / 1780 baht
Where: Seekantang Beach, 10-minute walk to Haad Rin
Address: 129/3 Moo.6, Haad Rin

Angkana Hotel Bungalows $$

Recharge your spiritual battery under the palm trees at Angkana's private beach resort. With only a handful of bungalows on this beachfront property, you can expect total peace and quiet. The entire resort is white sand, from reception to the shore – the sand is constantly being combed by the staff, creating this dreamlike world. Wade out into the still waters of the shallow bay and just sit in silence. Watch the occasional fisherman putter in with his day's catch and watch the sky change from bright blue to red and then orange.

Head back to your bungalow and sway the night away in your private hammock. Walk 15-minutes to Thong Sala Night Market or Thong Sala Town – an area with some of the best cafes and bistros on the island.

Starting at: $60 USD / 2000 baht
Where: Thong Sala
Address: Moo 2 Thongsala, Koh Phangan

The Coast Resort – Adults Only $$$

Charge up your camera, iPhone, mental camera, whatever…because this place is Instagram-worthy by definition! The Coast sits beachfront on the quiet end of Haad Rin under palm trees with sunset views! The bright red and orange bean bag chairs and pool umbrellas create a trendy "beach club" vibe – and the swim-up pool only adds to it.

When it comes to food, the pizza and house wine are to die for…and reasonably priced! When you want to party, just walk to the left on the beach. You'll come across a treehouse bar called "Escobar" and just a bit further than that are beach clubs, pool parties and the Full Moon Party beach.

The Coast is my #1 pick for a luxury resort that still has social vibes and party opportunities!

Starting at: $115 USD / 3770 baht
Where: Rin Nai Beach, 10-minute walk to Haad Rin
Address: 117/21 Rin Nai Beach

Where to Eat in Koh Phangan

Three Sixty Bar

The most incredible viewpoint on the island – and you don't even have to hike to see it! The name doesn't lie; Three Sixty Bar gives you jaw-dropping views of Koh Phangan's coastline including Mae Haad Beach. Take a seat on the wooden deck, order a cocktail, have a bite to each and just chill out. Stay for sunset or even later for that when the DJ starts heating up.

Heads Up: This bar is included in the Mingalaba Tour!

Pro Tip

Do not drive here yourself. The road is incredibly windy and steep. Take a Songtheaw and hold on tight.

Open: Daily 10.00 AM - 12.00 AM
Where: Koh Pha Ngan
Address: 85/2 Moo 7, Ko Pha Ngan 84280, Thailand

Soho

Draft beer and craft beer – oh, how I've missed you. For beer snobs, drinking Chang all week can get pretty old. At Soho, they feature local microbrews from the region – particularly from Cambodia.

They've got all your favorites on tap, too, like Carlberg and Tiger. If you're into sports, they've always got a match of some sort on the TVs and incredible Mexican food and western tapas to go along with the mood.

Open: 9:30am- 1:00pm
Where: Thong Sala
Address: 44/56 Moo1 Thong Sala

Amsterdam Bar & Restaurant

Over and over on the island, I heard "we're going to Amsterdam Bar" so I had to see what the fuss was about. So, imagine a beach club that isn't actually on the beach, but rather, in the jungle with insane views of the water and beach below. That's Amsterdam Bar. It's a viewpoint bar full of travelers lounging on mats on the floor with small tables and big portions of western food. There's a pool that no one really gets in, but it sets the mood – along with the live DJ. If you're looking to mingle – this is the place to do it. Be here for sunset – it's stunning from up here.

Open: Daily 12.00 PM - 1.00 AM
Where: Koh Pha Ngan
Address: Wok Tum, Koh Pha Ngan 84280, Thailand

Apichada View Point Bar

There are two things you must when you visit Apichada View Point Bar: either the big ass breakfasts or Khao Soi, which is an authentic northern dish that not many restaurants can do justice…but Apichada can.

If you're in the mood for a little house music and socializing, stay for their Sunset Parties where the viewpoint deck fills up with girls wearing flowers in their hair and guys who seemingly have forgotten to put on a T-shirt (totally not complaining).

Open: Daily 11.00 AM - Midnight
Where: Koh Pha Ngan
Address: Ban Tai, Ko Pha-ngan District

Rasta Baby

A sub sect of Thai culture seems to overlap with old school Jamaican culture. You'll find sprinkles of places like Rasta Baby with Bob Marley music, eclectic bartenders, beers with mellow prices, and Thai food that was made with lots of love for flavor. So, when you climb the stairs to reach Rasta Baby, plan on staying for a while.

Open: Daily 10am-2am
Where: Near Haad Rin
Address: Thong Nai Pan Noi Beach

Bite Delight

Yea, I know you came to Thailand to eat Thai food but seriously- if you consider yourself a foodie then you need to try some of this world-class cuisine. This candlelit Portuguese Wine Bar offers a wide selection of tapas like Bacon Croquettes, Gazpacho and an impressive Charcuterie Board. Order a few and you'll be stuffed.

Open: Sunday-Friday 6:30pm-11pm
Where: Ban Thai
Address: 64/9 Moo 2 | next to 7/11 Baantai

House People

Under a large, farm-style thatched roof with warm, dim lighting and plenty of space between tables, this is the place to come with that cute boy you met on the ferry. Ambiance is key, and the food certainly helps. Happy hour has some great drink specials to go along with your authentic Thai food cooked with just the amount of spice that you prefer.

Open: Sunday-Friday 3:30pm-11pm
Where: Had Yao/Secret Beach
Address: Haad Yao, Ko Pha Ngan 84280, Thailand

Vintage Burgers, Friends and Booze

Self-explanatory, right? Koh Phangan is the island of hangovers and what fixes a hangover best? Greasy fries and a juicy burger. Here, they go beyond beef. They've clearly had a lot of fun making the menu here with burgers ranging from ground chicken to vegetarian and vegan. Come and get it, girls.

Open: Daily 5pm-10pm
Where: Near the Ferry Pier
Address: Taladkao Road, Thong Sala, Ko Pha Ngan

Highlights & Activities

Slip N Fly

The best daytime party on the island, Slip N Fly proved that you're never too old to enjoy a waterslide…especially when it's 131 feet long. There's a massive pool with floaties and tanning spaces, plus drinks and a bar and boys and fun. Slip N Fly offers daily passes and Full Moon Party promotions so check out their website when you get to the island!

Starting at: $20 USD / 650 bath
Where: The middle of the island!
Address: 98/5 Moo 3 Madeuwan

Go Snorkeling
Just like Samui, you can build your own snorkel adventure or join a tour.

Option 1: By Beach
Rent a mask for the day and beach hop by motorbike. You're after the beaches with the most preserved coral and thus, the best underwater marine life.

- ✓ Mae Haad
- ✓ Chao Phao
- ✓ Haad Khom
- ✓ Koh Ma

Option 2: By Boat
Go into any tour office and ask about a snorkel boat trip! Just like Samui, you can join a bigger island-hopping tour like the Angthong Marine Park Day Tour that includes snorkeling but isn't all about snorkeling. Or pop into a dive center – their trips will be smaller and come with cute boys.

See the Sunset from the Secret Mountain
Get your blood pumping with a hike straight up Secret Mountain where you'll get a panoramic view of the entire island. Sunset is amazing from here! And there are tuk tuks at the top, waiting to drive you back down after your hike.

Literally any tour desk or even your hostel/hotel will offer this tour ranging anywhere from $30 - $50 per person.

Kite Boarding
Ban Thai Beach gets the perfect breeze for Kite Boarding conditions! There are at least four Kite Boarding schools along the beach with the full range of services from first timer lessons to gear rental for seasoned vets.

Cost: Starting at $118 USD /4,000 baht

Chill Out
Here, life begins and ends on the shore. Koh Phangan is the destination for lazy days and wild nights. Find a zen spot to catch some rays and splash about in the water until it's time for some nighttime antics.

The Best Tours

Mingalaba Island Tour

You'll drive almost the entire perimeter of the island in one day, stopping off at the best beaches, climbing up one of the most gorgeous waterfalls, and exploring a natural sand bar where you can snorkel! The last stop is Three Sixty Bar for instance views of the island and a drink. On the way back, the driver will keep his eye out for monkeys and stop if he's sees them. Hop out for a quick photoshoot.

All of this is done in an intimate group of 7 or 8 people in the back of a songthaew, making it easy to make some friends.

Responsible Traveler Tip

When you make your booking, emphasize that you DO NOT want to stop at the Elephant Riding Camp – and make the company confirm it. Visiting the camp is "optional" in the tour, so if people in your car ask to go there, the driver might oblige in order to receive a hefty commission from the camp.

The only way to end Elephant Riding practices is to refuse to participate.

How Much: Starts at $15 USD / 500 baht
When: 10am-3pm (roughly)
Where: Hotel Pickup

Explore the Waterfalls

The three most gorgeous waterfalls on Koh Phangan are Phaeng Waterfall, Paradise Waterfall, and Wang Sai Waterfall. Hire a tuk tuk driver to tour you around for a day of monkeying around.

Start off with the tallest Phaeng Waterfall, right in the center of the island. With just a 15-minute drive from Thong Sala Pier, you'll find the two connecting waterfalls that make up Phaeng Waterfall. If you're up for a 2.5-hour hike, you can follow the well-trodden path up to the waterfall viewpoint with stunning vistas of the entire island. Along the way you'll see monkeys and colorful birds. The hike isn't too strenuous, just long. So, bring some water, and then cool off in the waterfall pool afterwards.

The next stop is just a 5-minute drive north to Paradise Waterfall. You'll find a massive natural pool for swimming, playing on rope swings, and jumping from rocky ledges into the pool.

If you still got time to spare, definitely head farther north to the Wang Sai Waterfall where another natural pool surrounded by jungle awaits you!

Just like any other waterfall in Thailand, the best time to visit these places is during the wet season! I went in October and conditions were ideal. You can even go at the beginning of dry season and enjoy the leftovers from wet season.

Explore the National Marine Park

Over 40 tropical islands await you at Ang Thong National Marine Park. If you missed the opportunity to explore while you were on Koh Samui, it's no problem. You can take the speedboat tour from Koh Phangan and explore the entire park! See the hidden lagoons, the Emerald Green Lagoon Lake, coral gardens, white sand beaches, and even bizarre rock formations.

Markets & Shopping

Thong Sala Night Market – Koh Phangan

Thanon khon dern. Road person walk. That is exactly what you do as Thong Sala Night Market comes to life in the evenings, particularly on Saturdays.

The long and narrow road is packed with food stalls selling everything from Thai donuts to quail eggs. And in proper Thai fashion, you'll find every kind of meat on a stick, as well.

In the center of this walking street, there will be vendors on the ground who have laid out second hand t-shirt and toys, as well as, vendors selling leather purses, sparkly fanny packs and jewelry galore.

Pro Tip

Stay in the Thong Sala area on Saturdays so that you can walking distance to the madness.

Open: 4pm-11pm
Where: Thong Sala

Haad Rin Center

The cobblestone streets that run parallel to Haad Rin Beach are packed with shopping opportunities! For clothing, you'll find tons of stalls selling neon colored shirts and Full Moon Party gear. There are high end boutiques with lines dresses and crystal necklaces. You'll find pharmacies, 7-Elevens, mom and pop shops – you name it.

Haad Rin Pro Tip

Beware of the "Doctor Clinics" in Haad Rin. A friend of mine went in for an ear infection and came out spending nearly $400 USD. While the clinics in this area can diagnose you – for which you pay a doctor's fee of less than 1000 baht – they will severely overcharge you for medicine. SO, here's what you do: pay for the diagnosis, ask the doctor for the list of medication you'll need, go to a pharmacy and pick up your medications for a fraction of the price there.

Koh Phangan Nightlife

Infinity Beach Club

At any and every moment, you can walk outside your front door and find a party raging on Koh Phangan. Prime example: Infinity Beach Club. With 3 bars, 2 restaurants, and 1 big ass pool occupying 1,000sqm of prime beach front property- this place is alive at all hours of the day. Bring your suit and get ready to mingle. Happy hour is between 5-6pm for discounts on food and drink.

Open: 10am– 2am
Where: On Baan Tai Beach, 1 mile south east of Baan Tai Pier

Fubar

Traveling solo, right? Stop by Fubar any time of day or night and make some friends. The booze is always flowing, tunes are always going, and the bartenders are always up for a decent convo. They throw live DJ parties, partake in green activities and there's always a crowd ready to go bar hopping. You don't have to be a guest to join in on the fun.

Open: 24/7...yep.
Where: Right on Haad Rin Beach East

Ku Club

A legit nightclub on Koh Phangan, Ku Club is where you come to dance your face off past midnight. It's always packed thanks to seriously talented DJs, drink specials, and an inviting open-air venue.

Open: Daily 6pm-1am
Where: Baan Tai Beach
Address: The Beach Village

Koh Phangan Party Guide

 Full Moon Party

The famous Full Moon Party kicks off once or twice a month on Haad Rin Beach. It's such an epic party that backpackers and vacationers alike plan their entire Thailand vacation around this event. Expect tons of booze, dress in fluorescent colors, and I dare you to try and make it out of there without someone painting your face.

Solo Girl Tips for the Full Moon Party

✓ Book a hotel in Haad Rin so that you can easily get back to your hotel without relying on other people or transportation.

✓ Know that MANY hotels will require a minimum booking of anywhere from 2-5 days during the week of the Full Moon party.

✓ Expect hotel prices to be more expensive during the Full Moon party- it's annoying but consider it an investment in fun memories!

✓ Partygoers like to pop some fun pills here and smoke all sorts of weird stuff. Before you partake, make sure you are with a group of people who you trust and will stick with the rest of the night.

✓ Bring an over-the-shoulder purse and don't take it off. It's so easy to lose your bag at the Full Moon Party with all the chaos- so keep your belongings close.

✓ Watch your pockets as pick pockets prey on drunk people who have their guard down.

✓ Drink lots and lots of water. Write the word 'water' on your hand before you go out- especially if you plan to party hard. Water will keep you from blacking out and will keep you hydrated and healthy.

 **Waterfall Party**

Starting back in 2010, Waterfall Party has been rocking SE Asia with its massive electronic beats, gorgeous mountain views, and waterfall surroundings.

This event takes place twice a month (two days before the Full Moon Party, and two days after). Held deep in the tropical jungle of Koh Phangan, Waterfall Party has grown so popular that it now attracts recognizable international DJ's, fire shows, and acrobatic performances. Picture neon jungle, trippy glow-lights, an intense sound system, and dance party vibes! In short, if you love EDM, you want to go to this party!

And to feed all the jungle guests, there are food stalls, drink stands, market-style booths to buy jewellery and accessories for the party, and you can have yourself styled up by a professional body paint artist on site.

The party starts at 8pm and goes on for more than 12 hours. That being said, people do partake in psychedelics here…which I urge you not to do.

How do you buy tickets? You can purchase your ticket at the "door", or you can pre-book by visiting their **official website** – WaterfallParty.com

How do you get there? Jump in a songthaew. Most hotels, like Goodtime Backpackers, organize collective transport for their guests.

How much is it? 600 baht

- ### Solo Girl Tips for the Waterfall Party
  -
  - If you don't feel like doing the five-minute walk from the entrance of the jungle to the party area, there's a free lift service that'll take you there.
  - There are no ATM's on-site, so bring cash.
  - Things may get messy with paint and jungle, so don't wear your most expensive outfit or brand-new shoes!
  - It's 10 baht to use the bathroom here

 **Jungle Party**

Another massive event blaring deep house, tech house, progressive and techno music, Jungle Party is set in the middle of the Baan Tai Jungle. The feeling of this party is that of shared love for dance music, togetherness, and preserving nature! You know, hippie shit.

But this event is not only a massive dance party surrounded by awesome nature – it's also a circus-like event with live art installations, tons of glitter and sparkles, colourfully painted bodies, amazing costumes, and lots of smiling faces.

If you want to get "circus-y" too, there will be professional costume and body painting assistants, along with hair artists to make you look the part. For entertainment, expect Thai boxers showcasing their talent, extensive lights and lasers, and hula hoop fire dancers! It's wild.

The event takes place once a month, one day before the Full Moon Party, so if this sounds like your cup of tea, you best plan your Thailand adventure accordingly.

How do you buy tickets? You can grab a ticket at several backpacker hostels in Hat Rin and Ban Tai, or you can simply buy your ticket at the "door".

How do you get there? Jungle Party can be found in the Baan Tai Jungle in Ko Phangan. Like Waterfall Party and Full Moon Party, most party hostels will be organizing collective transportation where guests migrate together.

How much is it? 600 baht

- **Solo Girl Tips for the Jungle Party**
- Only bring what you're willing to lose. Make sure you leave your ATM cards at home.
- There is a first aid tent with qualified staff, free of charge.
- CCTV is available throughout the area.
- There are quiet zones and sleeping areas for those who want to chill
- Food and drinks stalls are available so bring some cash.

How to Get Around Koh Phangan

Not a Motorbike

I strongly do not recommend riding a motorbike on Koh Phangan. The roads are incredibly steep, windy and narrow with sandy patches that people wipe out on all the time.

Pair that with traffic and a collection of overconfident and sometimes, drunk travelers driving motorbikes and you've got tons of accidents.

Walk

If you're staying in the Haad Rin Area, everything you need is within walking distance! In fact, most beaches have a handful of restaurants and mom & pop shops within walking distance.

Songtheaw

Flag a Songtheaw down on the side of the road or have your hotel call one for you. On Koh Phangan, you're going to pay anywhere from 100 – 300 baht for a one-way ride.

Fun Thai Fact

There are over 8,000 7-Eleven stores in Thailand – with new ones popping up every week!

How to Get to Koh Phangan

 From Bangkok

 Fly to Surat Thani or Chumpon

If you're coming straight for Koh Phangan, the smartest way to do so is to a book a flight to either Surat Thani or Chumphon. These airports offer direct transports to the pier and shove you on a boat to the island.

 Take a Train to Surat Thani or Chumpon

If you're not pressed for time, the cheapest option to get to Koh Phangan is to take a train from Bangkok to Surat Thani. It takes 12 hours to Surat Thani and 8 hours to Chumpon, and then you can transfer to the pier easily from there.

 Take a Bus to Chumpon

If you can line up your bus with the ferry departures from Chumpon to Koh Phangan, the ferry is just 5 hours from Chumpon.

 From Phuket

 Fly to Surat Thani or Koh Samui

Then, it's a short boat ride from either place.

Ferry Routes from Surrounding Areas

✦ **From Surat Thani**

How Much: $20 USD / 650 baht
How Long: 2.5 hours
When: 7:00am - 4:30pm

✦ **From Koh Samui**

How Much: $10 USD / 300 baht
How Long: 30 minutes
When: All day long – last boat is usually around 7pm depending on the season

✦ **From Koh Tao**

How Much: $15 USD / 500 baht
How Long: 1.5 hours
When: All day long

Chapter 11: Koh Tao

The diving island! Koh Tao is famous for having incredible diving sites, world-renowned diving instructors, and is the most affordable place to become certified scuba diver with an Open Water Diving Course. This little island is a diver's paradise with over 50 diving schools. And as a close neighbor to Koh Phangan and Koh Samui, it's easy to add Koh Tao into your diving schedule.

When you're not diving, melt into the sand with a mojito in your hand while you watch unobstructed sunsets like you've never seen before. Beach bars are aplenty, as well as hotels and resorts. Dive hard, relax harder.

*But, party safely. Please read the Nightlife section before you come.

Island Breakdown

Sairee Beach
The main beach on the island! Sairee Beach is a mile-long strip of fine sand and a great spot for having cocktails while watching the sunset. Most nightlife occurs here but...again, be careful. Sairee Beach has a sinister history that most tourists know nothing about. In the daytime, Sairee Beach is welcoming and safe; but at night, there have been a few rare but serious crimes (See Koh Tao Nightlife).

Chalok Ban Khao
Enjoy some modern amenities without the crowd at Chalok Ban Khao Beach. Here you'll find several dive shops, a pharmacy and a 7-Eleven store. Not to mention, the beach is gorgeous.

Mae Haad Beach
Considered the capital of Koh Tao, everything you need is right here. Countless shops, restaurants, and bars are located at Mae Haad Beach. There are even ATMS and money exchanges.

Tanote Bay
Adrenaline junkies will find this beach alluring, albeit a little challenging to get to. Down a bumpy dirt road, only the dedicated adventurers make their way here. Tanote Bay is one of the best snorkeling spots with bright and beautiful corals, and this is also a spot for cliff jumping. *Just get travel insurance first, please!

Haad Thien
Haad Thien is one of the best beaches on Koh Tao. It's lined with coconut palm trees and water is crystal-clear. And the best part? It's not crowded at all because it's quite far from town. Stay at Haad Tien Beach Resort and you can wake up in paradise every morning.

Ao Leuk
Take a break from partying and head to this quiet beach with astonishing coral reefs. Travelers who love to snorkel prefer Ao Leuk.

Shark Bay
This private bay can only be accessed either by kayak or boat – and is totally worth the trip. The bay is gorgeous with fine white sand and clear water that offers amazing snorkeling with blacktip reef sharks. The best time to see the sharks is between 7 am and 10 am. You may spot some green turtles here too!

Accommodation in Koh Tao

Black Wood Hostel $

Located right next to the main pier and a 30-minute walk from the popular Sairee Beach, Black Wood Hostel is the perfect location to finish your trip before you jump back on the ferry. Every night, Black Wood Hostel offers a free cooking class (just have to pay for ingredients) where you can meet other tourists and learn a bit about Thai culture. Rustic, communal, and comfortable – staying here offers you that classic "traveler experience" you've been after all along.

Style: Dorms and Privates
Starts at: $7 USD / 250 THB
Where: Mae Haad Bay

White Jail at Koh Tao Hostel $

Weird name, super cool space -White Jail is the perfect balance between hostel and hotel with clean rooms *and* opportunities to meet other travelers. Get a chic private room or a tidy dorm room that offers you a decent amount of privacy. When you're ready to be social, go next door to the Jamaican Themed bar called "Rasta Baby" for music, dancing, and free BBQ every Friday night. The music does go til late so don't plan on going to sleep early.

Style: Dorms and Privates
Starts at: $10 USD / 300 THB
Where: Mae Haad Bay

In Touch Resort $

Direct beach access and a 2-minute walk from the best bars and shops- what else could you ask for? The main selling point of In Touch Resort is the beachfront deck where you can lounge on a floor mat under the trees while you watch the waves crash along the shore. Once you're all rested, the staff will help you arrange all of your boat tours and island adventures! Or you can simply wander across the street to SUP Tao Paddle Boarding and sort yourself out!

Style: Privates
Starts at: $67 USD
Where: Sairee Beach
Address: 1/16 Moo1, Sairee Beach, Koh Tao

Tanote Villa Hill

Tucked between jungle and palm trees overlooking the ocean, Tanote Villa Hill is breathtaking! Every single room has its own private balcony, and when you're located along a private beach, there is no bad view. The pools (yes, plural) mean that you never have to bump elbows with other vacationers or fight for a poolside lounge chair. After a full day of sunbathing, cool off at the bar or dig into a traditional Thai meal at the onsite restaurant. And if you're missing home, don't worry, they have a full western menu, too.

Style: Privates
Starts at: $97 USD/ 3,195 baht
Where: Tanote Bay

Sai Daeng Resort $$$

Wake up to views of the ocean from your private balcony, head down to breakfast with fresh tropical fruit, and then take a dip in the warm water. To get to this isolated resort with private beach, you can expect a free shuttle that picks you up at the pier (which you can arrange beforehand with the resort). Snorkel gear is free to rent, and the restaurant has plenty of amazing dishes to keep your palate entertained. This place is perfect for a little self-reflection where you can forget the world.

Style: Privates
Starts at: $118 USD / 4,000 baht
Where: Sai Daeng

Jamahkiri Resort

A perfect place to get away from the hustle and bustle of the center of the island, Jamahkiri Resort is located far enough to give you peace and quiet, but close enough for a bike adventure into town. If you don't want to spend the extra money renting a bike, just hop on their free shuttle when you want to go in town. Honestly, there's really no reason to ever leave the resort. Even the cheapest room comes with a sea view, and its prime real estate boasts a private beach perfect for snorkeling.

Style: Privates
Starts at: $173 USD/ 5,700 baht
Where: Shark Bay

Where to Eat on Koh Phangan

Koh Tao is a "walk and see" kind of eating scene. With tons of little sit-down Thai spots, picking random places to eat is part of the fun while staying on a small island.

But if you're looking to make lunch or dinner into an event, here are the must-try spots.

Barracuda Restaurant & Bar

Photo Credit: Barracuda Bar

Another popular seafood spot - Barracuda is where you can eat family style with massive platters full of shrimp, mussels, calamari, and fish that have been seasoned to perfection and served with homemade sauces that are to die for. So fresh. So worth it.

Where: Sairee Beach
Address: 9/9 Moo 1

Thaita Italian Restaurant
Take advantage of the abundance of fresh seafood with some killer ceviche at Thaita Italian Restaurant! Of course, you can find all of the Italian classics – handmade by Italians, might I add- such as gnocchi, Bolognese, and tiramisu. Every bite is next level!

Where: Sairee Beach – Next to Suksamarin Villas
Open: Daily 7pm-10:30 pm

251

VegetaBowl

After a week of stir-fried Thai food, your body will start to crave clean ingredients. VegetaBowl is fresh fresh fresh with salads, smoothies, and grilled veggies to replenish all the healthy nutrients your system craves. You can go full on vegan, vegetarian and dairy-free with every type of cuisine from Mediterranean with hummus or Japanese with handrolls! Pair with a fresh coconut and your body will thank you.

Where: Sairee, Near Ban's Diving
Ban Ko Tao
Open: Daily 11:30am-8:00pm

Seafood by Pawn

When you've got a Thai grandmother in the kitchen, you know that this Thai food is the real deal! Seafood by Pawn has got all the classics like whole grilled fish, som tam salad, and every curry dish under the sun. They also serve Beer Lao here- definitely a must if you're a beer drinker.

Where: Mae Haad Village

Highlights & Activities

Go Scuba Diving

Koh Tao is one of the cheapest places in the world to get your Scuba certifications.

This well-preserved island is a mecca for Scuba Divers- both brand new and experienced. Divers come from all over the world to swim with whale sharks, sea turtles, eels, and National Geographic-style schools of fish. You've got lots of options when it comes to dive shops-compare prices!

I got my certification with **Phoenix Divers**, who took me through a 4-day Dive Course with classroom training, pool practice, and the real deal – underwater dives. Another popular dive school is **Big Blue Dive School.**

Go Snorkeling

Koh Tao has some of the best snorkeling!
I won't bore you with filler here, I'll just tell you the best snorkel spots to go after when you're choosing a boat trip.

- Shark Bay
- Hin Wong Bay
- Mango Bay
- Aow Leuk
-

John Suwan View Point

John Suwan Viewpoint is located on the southern tip of Koh Tao, with stunning panoramic views of Chalok Baan Kao Bay, Shark Bay, and Thian Og Bay. It's a sea of crystal clear waters, green hills and palm trees!

From the base of the viewpoint, it's just a 15-minute hike to reach the top – with a 50 Baht entrance fee. Alternatively, you can hike up the 500-metre hill, accessible via Freedom Beach. Also, a 50 baht entrance fee. Neither hikes are too strenuous, but you will need to wear a pair of tennies.

How Much: 50 Baht
Best Time to Visit: Between 6:00 am for amazing sunrise views and less tourists.
Time Needed: Around one hour.

Visit Koh Nangyuan Island

Hop in a longtail boat on the west side of Koh Toa where you'll take a blissful 10-minute boat ride to the gorgeous shores of Koh Nangyuan. This beautifully peculiar strip of white sand beach connects three islands where you can climb, swim, and tan. Make sure to bring a camera- totally Instagram worthy. You can hire boats straight from the beach or have your hotel arrange a tour for you.

Ps. They close at 5pm.

Markers & Shopping

Wander the Streets

The cobblestone streets of Koh Tao are lined with shopping opportunities! Some of the best shopping (and bargaining) can be done here. Everywhere you turn, you'll find another clothing store or jewelry shack. There are also some western-quality dive stores selling fins, goggles, and dry bags.

Fun Thai Fact
Koh Tao was uninhabited until the 1940s, and the first resort was only built in the 1980s.

Koh Tao Nightlife

Be Aware: Sairee Beach has a sinister reputation. Full Disclosure: there have been murders, rape, and drugs in girls' drinks over the years, the most recent incident of drug and rape happening to a British girl in August 2018.

This behavior is extremely rare for Thailand, but a pattern on Sairee Beach – particularly at Leo Bar. **Do not go to Leo Bar.**

So, how do you stay safe and go out on Koh Tao?
Rule #1: No Bucket Drinks. Beers only.
Rule #2: Do not let your drink out of your sight!
Rule #3: Do not let a man buy you a drink.
Rule #4: Never *ever* walk on the beach past midnight, not even with a tall strong man who you think can protect you.
Rule #5: Be home by midnight.

Now that you're terrified (sorry 'bout that, sugar) – here's what you can do.

- Have some cocktails on the beach during the day and around dinner time.
- Watch the fire spinners on the beach and hang out with a big group of travelers
- Drink some beers and head back to your hotel by midnight

The predators on the island are Thai men looking for that solo backpacker girl who is in party mode and can be easily drugged.

The police aren't much help if something does go wrong, either. It's best to play it safe on Koh Tao.

Koh Tao Pub Crawl
The best way to meet other travelers and a few cute boys! The Koh Tao Pub Crawl hops from the best bars to the Ladyboy Cabaret to the beach for a fire show, collecting a free drink at each spot. The whole gang wears Koh Tao Pub Crawl tank tops (it's a unity thing, just go with it), and by the end of the night, you'll have made some new friends, gotten a decent buzz, and have gotten a lay of the land.

When: Every Monday, Wednesday, and Friday at 6pm

Where: Meet at Choppers Bar on Sairee Beach
How Much: $14 USD /450 baht

CoCo Bar

Sairee Beach's go-to party spot, CoCo Bar is a must-visit. This place is like a magnet for social creatures. Show up alone and you'll make friends within no time. Amazing cocktails and music that you actually want to listen to. Plus...there's always lots of cute boys here.
Where: Sairee Beach

Lotus Beach Bar

Grab a seat near the water's edge. Lotus has comfy floor tables and bean bags where you can sip cocktails with your toes in the sand while you watch Thai fire spinners perform some questionable, yet entertaining, stunts. Come for sunset and don't be surprised if you spend your whole night here.
Where: Sairee Beach

Good Vibe Bar

After a day of scuba diving and snorkeling, kicking your feet up with a really yummy cocktail and live music is the perfect way to end the day. Good Vibe Bar is more intimate than the raging beach parties, and you'll have a better chance of meeting some strangers and striking up a conversation – rather than getting wasted.
Where: Maehaad

Avoid Fish Bowl Bar and Leo Bar

Yes, it's the most popular party spot on the island...but this is where the majority of crime takes place. Don't let other travelers hype you up that this is a good idea, either. It's so easy to get swept up in the mood but you can find an even better mood elsewhere on the island. I pinkie promise.

How to Get Around Koh Tao

Motorbike

By now, you know that I don't recommend using a motorbike on Koh Tao or Koh Phangan. This is also not the place to learn how to drive a scooter with an island consisting of steep and risky hills. If you rent a bike here, use extreme caution. Rental shops require you to leave a passport or a very high deposit – because crashes are so common. Rentals start at 200 THB to 300.

Walk

The island is relatively small so almost everything worth visiting is within walking distance, via Koh Tao's cobblestone roads.

Taxi

Not really taxis, but pick-up trucks, rather. The trucks transfer you from piers to hotels and can also be hired to take you to viewpoints or other beaches on the island. However, they are expensive at 300 baht for a quick ride.

Getting to Koh Tao

 From Bangkok

 ### Fly to Surat Thani or Chumpon

If you're coming straight for Koh Tao, the smartest way to do so is to a book a flight to either Surat Thani or Chumphon. These airports offer direct transports to the pier and shove you on a boat to the island. It's so easy.

 ### Take a Train to Surat Thani or Chumpon

If you're not pressed for time, the cheapest option to get to Koh Tao is to take a train from Bangkok to Surat Thani. It takes 12 hours to Surat Thani and 8 hours to Chumpon, and then you can transfer to the pier easily from there.

 ### Take a Bus to Chumpon

If you can line up your bus with the ferry departures from Chumpon to Koh Tao, this is a great option as the ferry is less than 3 hours to the island.

 Ferry Routes from Surrounding Areas

✦ **From Surat Thani**

How Much: $24 USD / 800 baht
How Long: 5 to 6 hours
When: 9:00 AM - 11:00pm
*night boats take longer but save you money on accommodation

✦ **From Don Sak**

How Much: $20 USD / 750 baht
How Long: 4 hours
When: 10:00 am, 11:30am & 2:30pm
*night boats take longer but save you money on accommodation

✦ From Koh Samui

How Much: $20 USD / 750 baht
How Long: 2 hours
When: All day long

✦ From Koh Phangan

How Much: $15 USD / 500 baht
How Long: 1.5 hours
When: All day long

Section 4:

The Upper Gulf of Thailand

Region #3

The Upper Gulf of Thailand

Easy Term: The North

Includes:
- ✓ Pattaya
- ✓ Koh Chang

Best for...
- Scuba Diving Course

Known for...
- Gorgeous waterfalls and isolated beaches

Best time to Visit: November - April

Chapter 12: Pattaya

If you have limited time to spend in Thailand, maximize it by heading straight to Pattaya.

But before you go, I need to tell you something: Pattaya is the sex tourism capitol of Asia.

Yep. Lots of Thai prostitutes and fat white men.
And weirdly enough...lots of Chinese tourist – but that's not the point.

It isn't as grim as it sounds, however. What you'll see are tons of sports bars that look like old-man club houses where white guys drink cold beer, talk about sports, bitch about the economy and...are doted on by tiny, yet fierce, Thai women.

While it's gross, it's not dangerous for you. No one is interested in you...which is kind of liberating.

That being said, the only reason to come to Pattaya is to take a boat over to one of the gorgeous nearby islands: Koh Chang, Koh Kut or Koh Mak.

If you do want to spend some time in Pattaya, however, there are a few fabulous sites to see including one of the biggest floating markets in Asia.

I'm going to keep this chapter real brief and just point out how to use Pattaya as a jumping off point, and what to do with your layover time here.

Area Breakdown

Pattaya is super easy to navigate.

Pattaya Bay is actually just one long stretch of beach and the big town built behind it.

Pattaya Town, as it caters to mostly western men, has everything Western you could image from a Hooters to a Central Festival Mall to a McDonalds. And because of the large population of Thai women from small provinces in the North of Thailand (Isaan), you can also find some amazing Thai Food.

In Pattaya, you'll find a walking street, some shopping markets, and plenty of tour companies to jet you off to nearby islands. It's actually pretty convenient…just don't stay too long.

Accommodation in Pattaya

Viking Resorts $

With an emphasis on the cleanliness, Vikings Resort provides a unique experience with their basic, yet well-equipped rooms. The décor is so unique, tourists stop by just to take photos with the Viking Ship design in the front of the hotel. Guests love the complimentary breakfast and distance from the chaos of the center. It's trendy and cheap, and that's one of my favorite combinations.

Starts at: $25/ 823 baht
Where: 1 mile from the Centre
Address: 43/5 Moo10

The Bedrooms Hostel $$

Created with the name in mind, the Bedrooms Hostel is nothing like the typical. Each dorm room bed has its own private flat screen television, and remote. You'll forget your sharing with others until it's time to go out for the night and you suddenly have a squad of new friends to hang out with.

Starts at: $42/1383 baht

Where: 1 mile from the center
Address: 436/60 Moo 9 Pattaya Beach Soi 1

Achawalai Residence Village by Song $$$

Dedicated to making your trip as fabulous as possible, Achawalai Residence Village by Song does everything to make you feel at home. Of course, it's not so hard when the hotel rooms look more like apartments. The grounds are immaculate, with small gardens sprinkled through the property, ready for you to snuggle up with a book. If you're looking for an adventure, stop by the front desk to rent a bike – for free!
Style: Privates
Starts at: $90/2958 baht
Where: 5-minute walk to Jomtien Beach
Address: 365/62 Bun Kan Chana Rd., Na Kluea

Let's Hyde Pattaya Resort & Villas $$

A step above the competition, Let's Hyde Pattaya Resort and Villas will make you think you've got the wrong place considering how inexpensive their rooms are. The bed linen is high quality like the fancy hotels, with a top of the line restaurant, beautiful pool and simple access to a beautiful beach. There's nothing more you could expect from a four-star hotel.

Starts at: $59/1939 baht
Where: 5-minute walk Wong Amat Beach
Address: Soi Naklua 18/2

Pattaya Modus Beachfront Resort $$

Cut out the riff raff who are encroaching on your beach space! Pattaya Modus Beachfront Resort is a totally exclusive gated property where only hotel guests have access to the amenities, including the gorgeous pool and the private beach.

The other major selling point of Pattaya Modus Beachfront Resort is the location. Everything is within walking distance! A sacred temple is next door, a private beach is steps from your door, and the city center is only a short walk. If you want to splurge, there are even private pool rooms available!

Starts at: $79/2596 baht
Where: 5-minute walk Wong Amat Beach
Address: 381 Moo 5, Naklua Soi 12

Highlights & Activities

Pattaya Floating Market

Pattaya is home to the decade-old Four Regions Floating Market. It is the largest in the world, with over 114 vendors representing the whole country with colors and cultures from the four regions of Thailand. Spread across 100,000 square meters, spending a day here is an even it itself.

Traditionally, at a floating market, vendors row their boats through the canal while selling coffee, soup, and trinkets out of their boats. You can sit on the riverside and boat vendors will paddle up to you. Over the years, however, the boat vendors have been moving their shops on land for easier access to their customers. So, while you still can find some boat vendors keeping up with tradition – most of the shopping action is set up, traditional Thai-Market-Style, on the banks of the canals.

Wander through for some shopping of traditional Thai souvenirs. Relax with a massage. Fill your belly while sampling authentic curry, noodles (soup and stir-fry), sweet cakes and other local treats.

Getting there: Baht bus, motorcycle, metered or Grab taxi
Address: 451/304 Moo 12, Sukhumvit Road
Open: 10am-11pm
Entrance: 200 baht

Jomtien Beach Night Market – Pattaya

Up for a steady night out? Whether you are with friends or family, a stroll through Jomtien Beach and across to the other street to the market is exactly what you want to do. Despite being relatively smaller than the other markets, Jomtien sure garners a lot of positive reviews. Jomtien is well-known for its laidback and breezy atmosphere, good selection of reasonably priced food, great music, dancing and cleanliness. If you want to get away from the usual touristy hubbub, this is the place for you.

Where: Find the windmill between Soi Jomtien 8 and Soi Jomtien 9
Open: 5pm-11pm

Scuba Diving

Every day is diving day in Pattaya, and it has some of the best marine life that you're almost guaranteed to see turtles, stingrays, and a variety of sharks each dive! If you're lucky, you might even get to see a whale shark!

There are tons of diving schools here but if you want some place away from the crowd, head south to Jomtien and sign up at Jomtien Dive Center. They offer PADI courses with the standard recreational one priced at 14500 baht, inclusive of an online manual. This one is a 4-day course that starts you off at a pool and slowly trains you until you can do it off the boat. They also offer specialty courses like rescues and deep diving! You can check out more about their courses at their website.

Tiffany Cabaret Show

Spectacular and extravagant is what they describe the famous Tiffany's Cabaret Show, performed by beautiful ladyboys! The first in Southeast Asia and longest running transgender cabaret show started out in Pattaya, and it's voted as the top ten best shows in the world. Every night they have three shows, and you can now order tickets from various sites like Klook.

Wat Phra Khao Yai ("Big Buddha Hill")

Also known as 'Big Buddha Hill', Wat Phra Khao Yai is basically a temple on top of Pratamnak Hill with a huge and very obvious golden Buddha Statue. This 18-meter tall statue is the largest in the region, both locals and tourist alike go here to pay their respects. At the base of it, there are also other smaller Buddha statues in different positions as well as shops to buy souvenirs or incense.

Nearby Islands

 Catamaran Pattaya - Island Hopping
Check out the dive center called "Dive in Pattaya" that offers catamaran trips to the best beaches and islands nearby. At each island, you can hop off and snorkel with gorgeous fish in the pleasantly warm water. You'll go to islands like Koh Phai with white sand shores and Monkey Island / Koh Phet where money selfies are the thing to do.

Tour Package includes:
- Buffet lunch and drinks
- Snorkeling equipment
- Hotel pick-up and drop-off
- Towel

How much: Starts at US $69/2300 Bhat

 Spend a Few days at Nearby Islands
- **Koh Chang:** An amazing island for diving and waterfall treks
- **Koh Kut:** The 4th biggest Island in Thailand but with deserted beaches!
- **Koh Mak**: A tiny, middle of nowhere island perfect for off-the-beaten-path lazy days or curious adventures.

Pattaya Nightlife

Pattaya Walking Street

Every country has its red-light district and for Thailand, it is Pattaya Walking Street. Considered to have one of the best nightlife scenes in Southeast Asia, tourists and locals alike flock here to have all sorts of fun. The densely packed 1-kilometer strip is home to an endless stream of neon lights announcing clubs, go go's, open air bars and seafood restaurants.

Traveling solo? No worries as the place is considered generally safe. Be on the lookout for pickpockets though. While you are at it, consider playing a guessing game about the "ladies" that you see out there. Looks can indeed be deceiving.

Where: Soi 14 to Soi 16
Price: starts at 70-baht

How to Get Around Pattaya

Songthaew
"Wave and ride" is the way to go in Pattaya. While songthaews are legally required to load and unload passengers at designated stops, you will find that you can easily flag one down anywhere.

Grab Taxi
The easiest and safest way to get around Pattaya. Just download the app.

Taxi
Warning: metered taxis rarely use their meters and would negotiate for a fixed rate.

How to Get to Pattaya

 From Bangkok

Option 1: By Bus
Easily available from all over Bangkok!

Eastern Bus Terminal (Ekkamai), Northern Bus Terminal (Mo Chit 2 / Mochit Mai) Bus Station or Southern Bus Terminal (Sai Tai Mai).

How Much: Up to 5 USD / 150 baht
How Long: 2 to 3 hours
When: 5 AM to 11:30 PM

Option 2: By Minivan
From the same spots as above, minivans travel to Pattaya all day. I just find big busses to be more comfortable and typically drive at safer speeds.

How Much: 12 USD / 400 baht
How Long: 2 to 3 hours
When: 5 AM to 11:30 PM

Option 3: By Private Taxi
Your best bet is to use a website like KiwiTaxi.com and book a private taxi in advance. They can even pick you up from the airport and drive straight to Pattaya.

How Much: Up to 60 USD / 2000 baht
How Long: 2 hours

Chapter 13: Koh Chang

Attention: Adventure Seekers! Koh Chang is a scuba diving and waterfall chasing paradise! Here is your chance to do something different.

Koh Chang is this gorgeous paradise island with preserved coral reefs, dozens of jungle waterfalls, a thriving ecosystem, wildlife for days – and still has so many stunning resorts and welcoming guest houses. So why is it that there are no tourists here?

It's all about location! Koh Chang is nestled way off the mainstream travel path in Thailand. Located in the Trat region, Koh Chang is closer to Cambodia than it is Bangkok. Yet, it's still extremely easy to get to if you don't mind a few hours on a bus.

By the end of this chapter, you're going to be in love.

Island Breakdown

Koh Chang is a big island with plenty of popular and unnamed beaches to explore. Here are the areas that will help you plan your

adventure!

Lonely Beach

Locally known as Had Tha Nam, Lonely Beach used to only be accessible via one long hike. Lucky for you, there's now one single road that leads into it from Kai Bae. Still relatively undeveloped, this area is a backpacker's oasis! There's a walking street, humble accommodation and a welcoming community that knows how to have a good time once the sun goes down.

Bang Bao Pier

Located in the southwest end of Koh Chang, is this charming little fishing village built over water. It's a fun place to sightsee and got for a bite to eat, but the boats here are for fishing so, if you want to go snorkeling, head to the nearby Bang Bao Village.

Salak Phet Bay

On the southeast end of the island, you can find Salak Phet Bay. Here is the place to come for seafood and quiet beaches!

Klong Prao Village

A local area with local people, respectfully visit Klong Prao community for lunch and shopping. There is a traditional Thai temple here, so check your calendar and see what Buddhis holidays fall during your visit. If you're lucky, you'll be here during a temple festival which you're more than welcome to join.

The Northeast

There's a long stretch of beautiful unnamed beaches on the northeast side of the island filled with some of the best and most spacious resorts! Take the road less traveled and hike inland to discover the different waterfalls in the jungle.

Accommodation in Koh Chang

Pajamas Koh Chang $

If you're looking to ball out on a budget, with or without friends, pajamas Koh Chang is the best bet. They've narrowed down what they offer to ensure everything available to guests is top of the line. So, while there isn't a restaurant on site, there are weekly cooking classes, taught for free, and you get to eat your masterpiece at the end of the lesson. The facilities are super clean, and they even have a ping pong table, pool table, and guitar to keep you entertained when you're not in the pool or at the beach, which is just a 2-minute walk away.

Style: Privates and Dorm
Starts at: $17/558 baht
Where: 1-minute walk to Klong Prao Beach
Address: 18/22, Moo 4

Resolution Resort $$

Resolution Resort has gone above and beyond to create the best vacation experience on a budget. This place is located on prime beach real estate with direct beach access. There's palm trees overhead and jungle hills in the distance – all of which you can gawk at from their massive full-sun pool. They offer free boat rides, kayaks and have an adorable puppy on site to keep you company.

Style: Privates
Starts at: $57/1873 baht
Where: 1-minute walk hidden beach
Address: 50/5 Moo 1, Bang Bao Bay, Koh Chang Tai

Feel @ Chill Resort $

Located off the beaten path, Feel@Chill Resort Koh Chang is a hidden gem, offering guests peace and quiet, away from the tourist traps. Their café is top of the line, unlike their competition who tend to use instant coffee. Guests love hanging out in the common areas, surrounded by perfectly landscaped gardens, with friendly staff members eager to help you with bookings or even a motor bike rental to make the 10-minute ride to popular Long beach.

Style: Privates
Starts at: $36/1183 baht
Where: 500 m from Khlong Son Beach
Address: 20/1 moo3 Ban Khlong Son

Indie Beach Bungalows $$

If you've ever wanted to live the rustic life Thailand is known for, but you're a bit too prissy for the outdoors, it doesn't get better than the Indie Beach Bungalows. Designed it white and pastels, every room looks ripped from the pages of a fairy tale. If you really want to get the feel of living in a wonderland, opt for one for the bungalows equipped with a kitchen.

Style: Private
Starts at: $66/2170 baht
Where: 3-minute walk to Klong Prao Beach
Address: 32/3, Hat Sai Noi, Moo 1, Bang Bao

Nest Sense Resort $$

Next Sense Resort is more like a boutique hotel, only hosting a small number of guests which creates a more intimate and attentive stay. If you're checking out in the morning to make an early flight, don't be surprised if the staff wraps up your breakfast to take with you. They really know how to make you feel at home here. The pool is exceptional, with stunning views from all over the resort. Guests love the waterfall showers and supreme privacy afforded by the well-designed rooms.

Style: Privates
Starts at: $75/2465 baht
Where: 5-minute walk to Bailan Beach
Address: 188 Moo 1, Lonely Beach, Ko Chang

15 Palms Beach Resort $$$

The only difficult part about staying at 15 Palms Beach Resort is deciding if you like your hotel room better than the restaurant, which spills out onto the beach. I mean, there are bean bags in the sand for you to enjoy a freshly baked pizza, and I don't really know if life gets any better than that. But then, you'll see the room, some even have two levels, but each is super clean and well designed with modern finishes.

Style: Privates
Starts at: $98/3221 baht
Where: 1 minute from White Sand Beach
Address: 1/2 Moo 4, Baan Haad Sai Khao, White Sand Beach

Barali Beach Resort & Spa $$$

Just off the main road, Barali Beach Resort and Spa is just far enough to create a quiet atmosphere, without leaving you so far from the sites you need a taxi for everything. You can walk down the well-maintained beach to try out other restaurants, although there's one right on site for the nights you don't feel like going out.

Style: Private
Starts at: $145/4766 baht
Where: 3-minute walk to Klong Prao Beach
Address: 77 Kae Bae Beach, Ko Chang

Tantawan Resort Koh Chang $$$$

With private over the water bungalows equipped with their own kayaks, Tantawan Resort Koh Chang takes vacation to another level. Each room has a deep soaker tub, perfect for a relaxing evening after enjoying a day exploring. Resort staff can help you with booking tours to visit temples as well as snorkeling and boat trips. There's so much you can do, but I doubt you'll want to leave your room after you see the breathtaking view.

Style: Privates
Starts at: $205/6738 baht
Where: 5-minute walk to Long Beach
Address: Moo 3 Long Beach, Trat

Highlights & Activities

Go Snorkeling

Despite being the second largest island in Thailand, tourism is only fairly recent in Koh Chang, which means most of the marine and wildlife here are preserved and untouched

So, if you're not a diver or are a diver taking a break, go on an island-hopping snorkel trip!

Most boat trips are full-day trips that circle all the small neighboring islands like Koh Wai, Koh Rang, and Koh Lon - to name a few.

The bright, colorful fish and corals are scattered all around the island make for an exciting day of snorkeling and are an amazing opportunity for underwater photography! You'll see eels, angelfish, parrotfish, batfish, barracudas, triggerfish, and so much more!

If you're on the hunt for a bigger catch, there's also numerous sightings of moray eels, stingrays, sea turtles, and my personal favorite, whale sharks!

Check out any of the dive centers. They usually have the best information on where to find whale sharks and underwater life!

Koh Chang Diving Guide

What sets Koh Chang apart from the rest of Thailand's diving spots are the hidden gems under the sea —mainly in the form of shipwrecks and whale sharks! And, because Koh Chang is not located in a massive party zone, there has been less damage and erosion to the surrounding coral reefs. Koh Chang underwater world is unspoiled and waiting for you to explore it.

Across the island, there are tons of five-star PADI schools like BB Divers, the Dive Adventure, and Scuba Dawgs Koh Chang Dive Center. You're in good hands with them all.

To entice you underwater, here are some of Koh Chang's dive highlights.

- **HTMS Chang Wreck**

With a length of 117 meters, this is easily Thailand's largest wreck. You can already see it 5 meters down, but the captain's cabin lies 12 meters down. Keep going, the bottom deck is a harrowing 30 meters deep. This ship was sunk on November of 2012 and has since been developed as a large artificial reef with a diverse marine life with regular visits from groupers, barracudas, octopus, squid, and even whale sharks!

- **Hin Luk Bat**

This rock pinnacle is the most popular one in Koh Chang, not just because it's easy to access, but also because of the diverse marine life you'll spot here. Moray eels, stingray, parrotfish, butterfly fish, angelfish, barracudas, and best of all… dolphins! This is a great spot for beginner divers, with so much marine life living just 15 meters down. And an even better spot for night divers who get to experience the glowing Christmas Tree Worms!

- **T11 Wreck**

New divers almost never get to experience a shipwreck as wreck dives are reserved for more experienced divers – but here is the exception! T11 Wreck lies just 16 meters deep! The wreck is 30 meters long and lies horizontally at the bottom with the ship's cabins still totally identifiable. It may be small, but it's packed with marine life.

- **Thonburi Wreck**

Unlike the other two wrecks above, this has some history in it and wasn't intentionally sunk for reef life. A Thai warship was actually sunk by the French in 1941 due to a territorial dispute. Today, the Thonburi sits 15 meters below the surface and is covered in corals. It has its fair share of marine life, including barracudas, moray eels, and lionfish, but the actual ship is hardly visible now.

- **Koh Wai**

Feeling daring enough to face a shark? Head to this little island for the best chance of seeing reef sharks and leopard sharks!

Koh Chang Waterfall Guide

Koh Chang is famous for its mountainous terrain and thick forests, so that means tons of cliffs and hidden waterfalls to discover! Of course, there are already popular ones where most tour guides go to, but there are just as many unnamed waterfalls off the beaten path. Take note that some waterfalls have entrance fees, and they tend to dry up during the dry season.

Waterfall Tip

Hire a local to guide you on waterfall treks. Not only is this safer, but it's also the best way to discover the most hidden waterfalls.

Here are some of the best waterfalls on the island...

Klong Plu

Staying on the famous west-side beaches? Then you can head to the popular Klong Plu Waterfall just 1 kilometer from Klong Prao Beach. There are various climbing levels and platforms that range from 10 to 20 meters high.

Than Mayom

A 4-leveled waterfall that was said to be the favorite of two Thai Kings, Rama V and VII. You can even find their initials engraved on the rocks on the first and third levels. The bottom of Than Mayom is pretty shallow, so no diving here. It's still a popular spot for swimming, though! Pair your visit here with Klong Plu, as they're nearby one another and you can avoid paying for another entrance fee.

Klong Nung

The tallest and one of the most beautiful waterfalls on the island stands at 120 meters tall. Take caution as it's the least accessible (and potentially dangerous) because of the path to the top. Take a guide with you for the trek to the top where you'll be rewarded with beautiful views.

Kai Bae Waterfall

Here's a secret waterfall that you won't find marked on most maps or travel guides! It's rarely visited and hardly ever talked about but super easy to get to! From Kai Bae Beach, it's just a 30-minute walk from the hidden track behind a 7-11 on the south end of the village. Don't worry about getting lost because there are English signs that lead the way.

Klong Nonsi

Just behind the village of Dan Mai on the eastern side of Koh Chang is Klong Nonsi Waterfall, around 10 to 15 meters high. It's free of charge (aside from the parking fee), and a lot less crowded, too! Don't go during the dry season though because there's not much water left during that time.

Koh Chang Nightlife

Lonely Beach

Peaceful and serene during the day, you'd never guess that Lonely Beach turns into THE party spot at night. Lemon Bar used to be the #1 place to go for live DJs – now, they are just the warm up for Himmel Bar. Himmel Bar is the place you go to dance, have your ear drums blasted with super loud party tunes and flirt with some hot guys – cause sometimes that's fun.

You also might hear of Cancun Bar while you're on Lonely Beach. With an ideal location right one the beach, travelers flock here for bucket drink specials and live DJs in high season. You can party here until 4am and its good fun… BUT keep a straight head & always pay attention to your purse and your drink.

Kai Bae Beach

Filou Cocktail Lounge is the epitome of an island party – not too wild but wild enough – with live DJs and drink specials underneath a colorful tiki-style bar with a bar inside and an open-air patio for mingling outside. You've also go Mojito Lounge which really does live up to the name with great cocktails and more of a sophisticated lounge feel…great for a date!

Khlong Prao

Boom Bar! This quirky little pool hall has great live music – usually Thai-style reggae - and is the perfect place to go when you're traveling solo. The owners are engaging, the cocktails are trustworthy, and it's easy to chat up some strangers in this kind of atmosphere.

How to Get Around Koh Chang

Songthaew

This is the only public transportation available. This would not cover every area you may want to visit though.

Taxi

You can easily flag down taxis around town. There are pre-defined prices for the usual destinations. Make sure to ask the driver ahead of time.

Motorbike

While riding a motorbike or even a bike may be thrilling, always remember that steep hills and potholes abound in Koh Chang. Make sure to avoid any untoward accidents especially during the night.

How to Get to Koh Chang

 From Bangkok

Flying into Bangkok, there are now tons of ways to get to Koh Chang. You can choose to travel by land or take a flight - either way, you'll be heading to Trat before reaching Koh Chang.

Option 1: Flying to Trat Airport
In Bangkok (Suvarnabhumi) Airport, there are now four flights daily going to Trat Airport: morning, noon, midafternoon, and late afternoon.

How Much: $80 - $145 USD
How Long: 1 hour
For Booking: bangkokair.com

Option 2: Bus to Trat
If you're coming from the Bangkok Airport, the government 999 bus makes a stop here twice in the morning, with a few additional stops on the way. Free snacks are given out during the trip, though! It makes a stop at the two piers of Laem Ngop, which has a direct ferry to Koh Chang.

How Much: $8 USD (260 THB)
How Long: 5 - 6 hours

If you don't make the morning buses, there are buses from the Ekkamai Bus Terminal (Eastern Bus Terminal) directly to Trat, too. You can choose between a bus or minibus depending on how much leg room you want. Either way, there's going to be something available every hour from 4am to 11pm.

How Much: $8 USD (260 THB)
How Long: 6 hours

Option 2: Private Transfer to Trat

For groups, taking a taxi would be the cheaper option. Definitely not the choice for solo travelers on a budget, though. The best thing about this option is that it can pick you up at your hotel in Bangkok, too.

How Much: Around $140 USD / 4600 baht for 2-3 people, $155 / 5100 baht for 3-4 people, $170 / 5600 baht for 5-7 people
How Long: 4-5 hours
For Booking: kochangisland.com

 Ferry from Trat to Koh Chang

Once you reach the pier, getting a boat to Koh Chang is easy. The travel time depends on the kind of boat you get.

How Much: $3 / 80 baht
How Long: 30 - 45 minutes

Itineraries for Thailand

The biggest mistake I see girls making when planning a trip to Thailand is trying to see it ALL!

Thailand is huge and traveling between islands *can* take time. While trying to cover so many places and visit so many beaches in such short amounts of time, you end up rushing the most beautiful experiences.

Everyone you talk to about Thailand is going to have an opinion of where you HAVE to go and what you HAVE to see. Yeah yeah yeah, we get it.

Everyone cherishes their experiences, and naturally wants to share them with you. But then you just get overloaded with this massive checklist and now your vacation is a chore.

In order for you to have the best possible experience, you've got to be realistic with your time.

You've also got to choose the routes that are easiest to travel with regards to how many days you have in Thailand. After all, you don't want to spend half your trip in a bus.

So, here are some realistic itineraries to help you plan an unforgettable trip with just the right amount of activity to relaxation.

Want me to plan your trip for you?
Hotels, flights, and itinerary – I got you, girl.
Message me for trip planning packages at
Alexa@TheSoloGirlsTravelGuide.com

5 Days – Social Solo Girl

For the girls who want to party and make new friends from around the world!

Day 1: Phuket
- Fly into Phuket
- Settle into Bodega Resort or Lub D Hostel
- Go to a night market with fellow travelers!
- Get to bed at a decent time

Day 2: Phuket
- Get picked up in the morning by Elephant Nature Park for a full-day of elephant kisses.
- Back to your hostel
- Go for dinner with some fellow travelers
- Head to Bodega Resort at 9pm for the Phuket Pub Crawl

Day 3: Koh Phi Phi
- After breakfast, hop on a speed boat to Koh Phi Phi
- Check into your hotel and go exploring!
- Get rid of that hangover with a tanning nap at Hat Laem Thong Beach
- Eat dinner and socialize at Banana Bar
- Head to Loh Dalum Beach for sunset and fire spinners

Day 4: Koh Phi Phi
- Head to the beach for some morning zen and a swim
- Island Hop with Phi Phi Pirate Boat Booze Cruise
- The rest of the night is a guaranteed mystery

Day 5: Koh Phi Phi
- Get rid of that hangover with a hike to Phi Phi Viewpoint
- After your workout, reward yourself with Ibiza Pool Party
- Take an evening boat back to Phuket
- Have one more Thai massage and stock up on all the souvenirs before you fly home!

1 Week: Active Adventure Babe

Day 1: Krabi
- Fly into Krabi Town.

- Stay at a villa near Ao Nang Beach.
- Have lunch at Krabi Cafe 8.98
- After a long flight, relax with your first Thai massage!
- Head over to Krabi Town Night Market for some people watching, beer drinking, and street food eating.

Day 2: Ao Nang Beach
- Sign up for a morning Kayak Tour through the mangroves
- Come back and have a pool day
- Go to The Last Fisherman's Bar for sunset dinner and cocktails.
- Wander Ao Nang's boardwalk with Thai street shopping and hole in the wall bars

Day 3: Ao Nang Beach
- Rent a motorbike and drive to Tiger Cave Temple for a morning hike to the top
- Drive to the Emerald Pool and Hot Springs
- Come back to your hotel and collapse
- Eat local street food

Day 4: Railay
- Take a quick long-tail boat over to Railay Beach.
- Check into your new accommodation
- Head over to Tonsai for a 2pm- 6pm Rock Climbing course
- Have dinner at Family Restaurant

Day 5: Railay
- Spend the morning at the beautiful Phra Nang Cave Beach
- Hop on Krabi Sunset Cruise – leaving at 1pm!
- Dinner onboard the boat!
- Freshen up at your hotel
- Then head over to Railay East, where the Krabi Sunset Cruise crew will be partying and watching Muay Thai

Day 6: Koh Lanta
- Jump on a boat to Koh Lanta
- Rent a motorbike and have a relaxed day of beach hopping

Day 7: Koh Lanta
- Up early for the 4 Island Tour to Emerald Cave

- Have dinner at Surya Restaurant & Bar, watch the sunset while you eat

Day 8: Koh Lanta & Back
- Go on a morning tour to Khao Mai Kaew Caves
- Head on an afternoon ferry to Phuket/Krabi for your flight home!

2 Weeks: Mermaid

Mermaids, you'll be in your bathing suit every day!

Day 1: Koh Samui
- Fly into Koh Samui and stay on Chaweng Beach
- Put on your suit and head straight to the beach for a swim
- Do a little street shopping, then have dinner at Green Bird
- Head to Ark Bar for sunset and fire spinners
- Get to bed at a decent time!

Day 2: Koh Samui
- Up early for Ang Thong Marine Park Day Tour
- Snorkel and explore some of the last virgin islands on earth
- Head for a Thai Massage after your boat tour
- Experience Starz Cabaret in the evening

Day 3: Koh Samui
- Visit Lamai Beach in the morning – sightsee at Grandmother & Grandfather Rocks.
- Put your suit on for Ark Bar pool party in the afternoon
- Have a quick bite to eat at The Islander
- Go to a Muay Thai Fight in the evening

Day 4: Koh Samui
- Move hotels – up to Sensimar Resort
- Have an infinity pool day and socialize at the pool bar
- Zen out on the gorgeous Mae Nam Beach
- Check to see which night markets are near you or head to Silent Beach for happy hour.
-

Day 5: Koh Phangan
- Take a ferry over to Koh Phangan

- Check into your hostel or resort
- Explore the beach nearest to you!
- Head to Jungle Bar or Amsterdam Bar for sunset

Day 6: Koh Phangan
- Up early for the 10:00am Mingalaba Island Tour
- Explore Haad Rin's party area at night!

Day 8-12: Koh Tao
- Jump on a ferry to Koh Tao
- Head to Phoenix Divers for a 4-day Open Water Scuba Diving Course

Day 13: Koh Tao
- You've earned a day off – lounge on Sairee Beach all day or explore Tanote Bay
- Order a coconut and tan
- Go to Dinner at Barracuda!

Day 14: Back Home
- Jump on a boat to Surat Thani or Koh Samui and fly home!

2 Weeks: Island Hopping

Day 1: Fly into Bangkok
- Take a bus or taxi to Trat
- Take a ferry to Koh Chang
- The next few days are going to be so simple, go with the flow for an unforgettable and carefree experience.

Day 2: Koh Chang
- Rent a motorbike and go beach hopping
- Use the Waterfall Guide and discover some waterfalls
- Get a massage in the evening!

Day 3: Koh Chang
- Sign up for a snorkel trip or scuba diving adventure
- Explore Koh Chang's nightlife on Lonely Beach

Day 4: Koh Chang
- Take a cooking class!
- Pick your favorite beach for a lazy afternoon with a book

Day 5: Koh Tao
- Take a minivan and ferry to Koh Tao (book with 12Go.Asia)
- Head to Sairee Beach for sunset
- Sign up for the Koh Tao Pub Crawl

Day 6: Koh Tao
- An active day! Hike to John Suwan View Point in the morning
- In the afternoon, jump in a longtail boat and visit Koh Nangyuan Island
- It's time for Thai massage #2

Day 7: Koh Tao & Koh Phangan
- Up early! Hop in a long tail boat to Shark Bay and snorkel with sharks!
- Take an afternoon ferry to Koh Phangan
- Check into The Coast resort and enjoy the infinity pool & pizza
- Wander down the beach to EscoBar

Day 8: Koh Phangan
- Up early for the Mingalaba Island Tour at 10am
- Hit up Happy Hour at Infinity Beach Club and then go clubbing at Ku Club

Day 9: Koh Phangan
- Take a cooking class in the morning
- Spend the afternoon at Slip N Fly or find a beach to collapse on!
- Wander Haad Rin and eat local

Day 10: Koh Samui
- Jump on a boat to Koh Samui
- Check into your new hotel in Fisherman's Village, The Waterfront Boutique Resort
- Put your swim suit on and head directly for the sea!
- Have dinner, cocktails and enjoy the view
- Find a nearby night market to explore

Day 11: Koh Samui

- Sightseeing day! Rent a motorbike or hire a driver for the day
- Visit Wat Plai Laem Temple and Wat Phra Yai, and Grandmother & Grandfather Rocks
- Take a break at Lamai Beach and the pristine white sand
- Have a Thai lunch/dinner at The Black Pearl
- Walk the Fisherman's Village Walking Street until you make it to Coco Tam's Beachfront Bar
- Chill out
-

Day 12: Koh Samui

- Sign up for Ang Thong National Marine Park Island Hopping Tour
- Eat dinner at RockPool Restaurant
- Experience Starz Cabaret Show at 9:45pm

Day 13: Koh Samui

- Change hotels, down towards Chaweng or Lamai
- Spend the day at Ark Bar's pool party
- Go back to your hotel and freshen up
- Return to Ark Bar for dinner, sunset, and fire spinning and cocktails

Day 14: Koh Samui

- Hop on a quick 3-hour ferry back to Surat Thani to catch a flight to Bangkok or fly directly from Koh Samui to Bangkok.

Alternatively- you can do this loop in the other direction. Up to you!

Just want me to plan the whole damn thing for you?
All I need is your Thai Bucket List.
Reach out to me at **Alexa@TheSoloGirlsTravelGuide.com** for trip planning packages.

Thai Food Guide

There's more to life than just Pad Thai...

Tom Yum - A spicy and sour lemongrass soup, often served with shrimp

Tom Kha Gai- Hot and sour soup with coconut & kaffir lime leaf base served with chili, mushrooms, and chicken

Penang Curry- My #1 recommended curry dish that is sweet and fragrant with lime kaffir lime leaves, basil and coconut.

Gang Kiew Wan Gai- Green curry with chicken served with steamed rice

Massaman Curry- A southern Thai curry with a peanut and potato broth served with steamed rice

Khao Man Gai– Hainanese chicken and rice served with a simple chicken broth

Pad Ga Prow Moo (kai dow)- Chili basil stir-fried pork (with a fried egg on top)

Pad See Ew- Wide rice noodles stir-fried in soy sauce with broccoli and protein (chicken, seafood, pork)

Som Tam- Green Papaya Salad with dried shrimp

Pla Kapong Neung Manao- A whole steamed bass with lemon and chili in a shallow broth, often served at the table over fire.

Khao Ka Moo
Stewed, fall-off-the-bone pork leg topped with rice and rich pork broth

Kow Neuw- Sticky rice

Khao Soi- A Burmese/Laos inspired soup made with coconut milk, red curry paste, yellow egg noodles and topped with crispy wonton strips

Kanom Krok- Little fried pancakes with a crispy shell

Kow Neuw Mamuang (Mango Sticky Rice)- Sweet and salty coconut sticky rice served with fresh mango

Kanom Tuay- Layered sweet and salty coconut dessert pre-set in tiny bowls

Thai Festivals and Holidays

February

 ✦ Chinese New Year

When: February 5th, 2019

Year of the Dragon will be celebrated in Phuket, namely the "Four Old Streets" of Thalang Road, Krabi Road, Dibuk Road and Phang Nga Road. In past years, these streets are closed to traffic and parades are held with firecrackers and gongs and parades!

While the firecrackers and parades are fun …I have to warn you!!! Thailand is a massive vacation destination for the Chinese right now. With a full week off in China, you can expect an influx of tourists to Thailand. Particularly to Phuket and Koh Samui.

My Suggestion: Head for the smaller islands on February 5th and stay a few days.

April

✦ Songkran Water Festival | Thai New Year

When: April 13th-April 15th, 2019

Thailand's water festival is one of the biggest holidays of the year for both Thais and tourists. The water fight madness represents cleansing for the New Year in hopes for a bountiful harvest. For 4 days- you can't leave your hotel without getting soaked by water guns or strangers dumping water over your head. It's wild.

Most Popular Celebration Spots:
- Chaweng Beach, Koh Samui
- Patong, Phuket (Bodega Hostel)

July

✦ Vassa | Beginning of Buddhist Lent

When: July 28th, 2019

Although Buddhist lent lasts into October, on July 28th, you will find temple celebrations at any temples that celebrate Buddhist culture. At major temples around Thailand, you can witness candle making, flower ceremonies, and parades- all of which welcome tourists to participate. PS: Bars will be closed so you might as well join in.

October

✦ The Anniversary of the Passing of King Bhumibol

When: October 13th, 2019

Thailand lost their beloved King Bhumibol in 2016. He was loved and respected deeply – and is considered the father of this country. On October 13th, Thai people will wear black in commemoration and there will be a moment silence held across the country at 3.52pm. It's not always for sure, but there's a strong chance that alcohol will not be sold on this day.

Most Popular Celebration Spots:
- Bangkok – The Grand Palace

✦ Loi Kratong | The Lantern Festival

When: November 13, 2019

This Buddhist holiday represents the birth, enlightenment, and death of Buddha- and is celebrated nationwide. You may be familiar with how Loy Kratong is celebrated. Thousands of glowing lanterns are released into the sky...but not on the islands of Thailand – you'll have to be in Chiang Mai for this. However, there are temples and lakes on the islands that will release floating lanterns into the water. These locations change every year but once you're here, celebrations will be advertised!

Most Popular Celebration Spots:
- Chiang Mai- Ping River or Nawarat bridge
- Bangkok – Bejakitti Park

December

✦ Western New Year

When: December 31st – January 1st (duh)

You can find fabulous parties in any major city or beach town in Thailand! Expect glittery dresses and drink specials just like back home.
Most Popular Celebration Spots:
- Expect the typical party beaches to throw epic parties!

Safety in Thailand

A quick briefing...

* ❖ Violent crime against tourists is rare.
* ❖ Crime here typically comes in the form of scams rather than actual danger.
* ❖ Assaults typically happen between two travelers, rather than a traveler and a local.
* ❖ It is safer to walk in Bangkok at night than it is to walk in Seattle at night.
* ❖ Use street smarts like you would back home and you'll be fine.
* ❖ Koh Tao is an exception to all of the above! Check out the Koh Tao Nightlife Section for details.

Wear a Cross Shoulder Bag
Although theft is not a huge issue over here, it's always better to play it safe. No one would be dumb enough to try and pull a cross-shoulder bag off of you. At least, not in Thailand.

Look Both Ways Before You Cross the Street
Duh, but really- traffic here is different than back home. Pedestrians don't have the right of way here- even on a green light. When crossing the street, don't just look for cars- look for motorbikes that whiz between the cars, too!

Walking at Night
Make smart choices. Stay on lit roads, don't walk down a dark beach late at night, walk with a friend when possible, and don't get super drunk and wander off by yourself. Follow those commonsense rules and you'll be fine.

Use ATMs inside Convenience Stores
As a universal travel rule, ATMs inside supermarkets, convenient stores, and banks are your biggest insurance policies against becoming a victim of using a fraudulent ATM or having a wad of cash ripped out of your hand - although, I've never heard of either of these things happening in Thailand).

Bucket Drinks + "Fake" Alcohol = Wicked Hangover
It's a common scam: Thai vendors will concoct homemade alcohol and pour it into name brand bottles; usually the white stuff like gin and vodka.

Bucket drinks are staple island parties and you'll be offered buckets everywhere you go. While you're not likely to experience liver failure after one of these drinks, you are certainly going to experience an intense hangover. Stick to beer – unless you're drinking at a reputable hotel or hostel. Bodega Hostels, LUB D and pretty much any accommodation in this guide is safe on the alcohol & buckets front.

Beware of Sneaky Bartenders

When paying bartenders, make sure you say out loud "Here's 1000 baht" or "500 baht" to make sure they can't claim that you paid a lesser amount – which they've been known to do in party areas in hopes that you're too drunk to notice.

Let's Talk about Sexual Assault

Foreign women (that's us) are statistically more likely to be sexually assaulted by a foreign man (other travelers) on holiday than they are to be sexually assaulted by a Thai man. Think about it; in hostels, hotels and bars- we are more likely to be hanging around foreign men, quite possibly with alcohol in our systems, and therefore exposed to that risk. Just like you would at home, monitor your sobriety levels and be aware of your surroundings.

Gem & Jewelry Store Scams

In Thailand, the most common scam is one where a tuk tuk or taxi driver takes you to a jewelry store where they get commission if you buy. It's annoying and a waste of time, but not dangerous.

Here's how they get you…

- ❖ "Closed today" Declarations: If you want to go to a temple and the tuk tuk driver tells you that the temple is closed or opening late today due to a "Buddhist Holiday" …they're lying and are trying to get you to a jewelry store.

- ❖ 20 Baht Rides: If a taxi driver offers you a suspiciously low rate for a day of sightseeing, expect to pass all the tourist destinations and be taken straight to a jewelry store.

Other Tuk Tuk Scams

Rule of Thumb: If a tuk tuk driver takes you to ANY place other than the place you have requested – they are scamming you.

❖ Government Travel Agencies aren't a thing and they won't give you a better deal – don't let a driver tell you otherwise.

❖ "Stopping for lunch" means "I'm taking you to my friend's shitty restaurant, so I can make some extra cash"

✦ In conclusion! As foreign women, we can expect to feel safe in Thailand as long as we use common sense and don't get too wasted. It's really as simple as that.

What to Pack for Thailand

First. Don't stress. As long as you have your passport, bank card and a decent backpack- you're ready for Thailand. Anything you need or forget at home can be found in somewhere on these islands- just at a slightly more expensive price.

So, let's get organized now. It's taken me years to perfect packing for Asia, but I've finally got it down. This list will help you out tons!

The Perfect Backpack

Yes, backpack! Not a rolley suitcase. With sandy beaches, the absence of sidewalks, and dirt roads with potholes, you want a bag you can easily carry on and off a boat. Even more important, there is no free checked baggage on short flights – you need an overhead compartment sized bag unless you want to pay $30 to check a bag.

My go-to backpack is the **Osprey Farpoint 55** or 40-liter bag. I've gone through several backpacks over the years, and this one is my golden child.

Walking Shoes

Bring 3 pairs of shoes
- ✓ 1 Pair of Flip Flops
- ✓ 1 Pair of Cute Walking Sandals
- ✓ 1 Pair of Hiking / Running Shoes

This is my magical trifecta of shoes. Through rain, up mountains, and on long sweaty walks, they've never failed me. I replace the same pairs of shoes every year – find them in my travel store.

Electric Adapter

Your phone, laptop and computer are likely not going to be compatible with the Thai outlets. REI, Target, and Amazon have cheap Universal adapters that every traveling girl should own

Tampons

Thai girls don't use tampons; they use pads. And pads don't work with a bathing suit, now do they? You can find tampons over here but they are more expensive and will have 1 option/style per store.

Empty Space in Your Bag

It took me 5 years to learn that the less stuff you have, the more free you are. You are free to pick up and move around, free to shop for souvenirs, and free from relying on porters and taxis to help you carry your luggage.

Emergency Money Source/ $100 Cash US

Have a secret stash of cash or a backup credit card in case you get in a sticky situation. Keep this emergency money source separate from your other cards and cash- so that if you lose your wallet, you won't lose the secret stash, too.

Quick Dry Towel

Hostel girls! Hostels usually don't provide towels so it's nice to bring a travel towel of your own. Not a total necessity, but a quick dry (usually some kind of microfiber) towel is nice to have- especially during rainy season when the heat isn't there to dry things quickly. Plus, it can double as your beach towel! Normal towels are too bulky and take forever to dry- so don't bother bringing one.

Passport with at Least 6 Months Validity

Some countries enforce it and some countries don't- but to play it safe, you need to have at least 6 months validity on your passport. For example, if it's January 1st, 2019, and your passport expires before June 1st, 2019, they might not let you in the country and you'll have to return home immediately.

Bank Cards

Travel with two. In the case that your bank flags one card with fraud and disables it, you'll want to have a backup. If the machine eats a card, if a card gets stolen, or if you lose your purse on a night out, a backup card will make all the difference between having mom fly you home and you continuing your travels.

Travel Insurance

Better safe than sorry. From minor bouts of food poisoning to helicopter medevac off a mountain, a standard travel insurance policy is a nonnegotiable in my (literal) book. Check out a company called **World Nomads** which offers full-coverage plans for extremely reasonable prices.

What NOT to Pack

- ✓ Jeans
- ✓ Hairspray (ya won't use it)
- ✓ High-heels
- ✓ Anything Aerosol
- ✓ A Pharmacy of Medicine
- ✓ Too Many Bras (ya won't wear em')

Want to see what I travel with?

All of my favorite travel must-haves can be found in my Travel Store
at HowToTeachInAsia.com

Tourist Visas for Thailand

Three Options for Tourist Visas for Thailand

1. Visa on Arrival via Air

Fly into Thailand and get a 30-day stamp in your passport- no need to prepare a single document.

2. Visa on Arrival via Land

Cross into Thailand by land and get a 30- day stamp in your passport- no need to prepare a single document.

*Occasionally, instead of a 30-day visa, Thai immigration will change this tourist allowance to a 15-day visa when crossing over via land. It doesn't happen often but has happened in the past. Double-check with your Thai embassy's website if you plan to enter Thailand by bus or taxi.

3. 60-Day Tourist Visa

Before you come to Thailand, you can go to the nearest Thai Embassy and apply for a 60-Day tourist visa. You can do this in any country where there is a Thai Embassy- it doesn't have to be your own country.

It costs about $60 USD & you'll need to have proof of an exit flight. Don't have an exit flight? Check out BestOnwardTicket.com for a temporary exit flight.

Bonus: The 60-day Tourist Visa can be extended an extra 30-days (equaling 90-days total)! You can extend this visa while in Thailand, starting 7 days before your visa expires.

Example: My 60 days expires on June 7th. So, I can go to immigration on June 1st (or any day in-between) to renew. Closed on Sundays! Skip Saturdays, too.

To do this, go to the nearest Thai immigration office and pay an extra $60 USD/$2,000 baht along with proof of an exit flight.

These rules apply for tourists coming from western countries such as Canada, The UK, South Africa, The USA, Australia, and Ireland. If you live elsewhere, the rules may be different for you so check your local Thai embassy website.

Quick Thai Lesson

Girls end every phrase with: Kah
Boys end every phrase with: Kap

 **Greetings**

Hello - Sa-wa-dee-kah
How are you? - Sa-bai-dee
What's your name? - Kun chêu a-rai?
My name is… - Rao chêu …
Nice to meet you - yin dee têe dâi róo jà
Where's the toilet? - hông náam yòo nǎi?
Bye – Bye

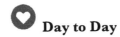 **Day to Day**

No Problem – Mai pen rai
Whatever (doesn't matter) – A rai ga dai
I don't know - Mai ru
I don't understand – Mai kow jai
Please say that again - pôot èek tee dâai mǎi
Please speak more slowly - pôot cháa long nòi
How do you say ____ in Thai? - pasa tai … poot waa yàng-rai

 **Shopping**

How much? – Tao rai?
I want ____ - Ow ____
I **don't want a bag** – Mai ow tung
Big – Yai
Small – Lek
I like it – Chan chok man

Food

Delicious – aròi
Chicken - Gai
Pork - Moo
Beef- Neau
Fish/Shrimp- Plah/Goon
Vegetarian – mang-sà-wí-rát
Rice – Khao
Coconut – Maprao
Spicy- Pet
I'm hungry – Chan hew
I'm full – Chan im

Emergency Phrases

Leave me alone! - Yā yung kap chan!
Help! – Chuay Duay!
Fire! – Fai mâi!
Stop! – Yut!

Want to practice your Thai Language skills before you go?
Take a "Survival Thai" course with me over Skype!
Make friends, save money in markets, and order exactly what you
want at restaurants with just a little bit of Thai in your repertoire.

Email me at Alexa@TheSoloGirlsTravelGuide.com

Directory

Tourist Police – English Speaking
Phone: 1155 (free call from any phone) or 678-6800
Address in Bangkok: TPI Tower, 25/26 Liab Khong Rd., Chong
Nonsi Junction, New Chan Rd.

American Embassy
Emergency Line: 02-205-4000
Address: 95 Wireless Rd Khwaeng Lumphini Pathumwan

British Embassy
Emergency Line: 02 305 8333
Address: 14 Wireless Road Lumpini Pathumwan

Canadian Embassy
Emergency Line: 02646-4300
Address: 15th Floor, Abdulrahim Place 990 Rama IV Road Bangrak

South African Embassy
Emergency Line: 02659-2900
Address: 12th A Floor, M Thai Tower, All Seasons Place, 87 Wireless
Road, Lumphini Pathumwa

Australian Embassy
Emergency Line: 02 344 6300
Address: 37 South Sathorn Road
Tungmahamek, Sathorn

Doctor Mac - Apple Repair
For Broken Apple Products
Phone: +66 82 279 8746
Address: 115/9 Moo.6
Open: Daily 10:00am – 8:00pm

Pro Tip

When calling from outside of Cambodia with an international
number (anything other than Cambodian), add the country code
(+855) and make sure you've dropped the first 0. When calling with a
Cambodian number, drop the country code and add a 0.

For example: +855 23 427 124 = 023 427 124
Same number. Different input.

OB/GYN & Female Stuff

Birth Control
You can buy birth control pills and contraception over the counter in Thailand
Where: All pharmacies and Boots Drug Stores

Morning After Pill
Where: Every pharmacy carries it under "Postinor" or "Madona" for 40-60 baht

IUD Birth Control
In Bangkok, you have access to high-class doctors with prestigious training at a fraction of the price back home. Get your IUD here.
Where: Vejthani Hospital, Bangkok
How Much: $300 USD for IUD and insertion. Transport included.

OB/GYN Centers of Thailand

Women's Center (OB/GYN) | Bumrungrad Hospital Bangkok
All of the services including birth control, ultrasounds, STD testing, etc.
Open: Monday through Friday 7am to 8pm/ Saturday 7am to 7pm/ Sunday 8am to 8pm
How to Get There: BTS Nana
Address: 33 Soi Sukhumvit 3

Unwanted Pregnancy - Klong Tun Medical Center
Open: 24/7
How to Get There: BTS Phra Khanong- Next to Cabbages and Condoms Restaurant on Sukhumvit 12
Address: 3284 New Petchburi Road Bangkapi Khet Huai Khwang
Phone: 02 319 2101

Bangkok Hospital Phuket - International Hospital | Dr. Kittipat Pongpech
Open: Daily 8am to 5pm
Address: 2 1 Soi Hongyok Utis, Tambon Talat Yai
Contact: +66 7625 4425 or visit their website.

Medical Tourism is catching on in the USA.

People are understanding that going abroad, to places like Thailand where medical standards are extremely high, is a cheaper alternative to receiving medical care at home.

- ✓ Fertility
- ✓ PAP Smear
- ✓ STD Testing
- ✓ Birth Control

Consider making your trip a dual-purpose vacay for medical, dental or cosmetic procedures! Now your airplane ticket is so easy to justify!

For more information, check out gynopedia.org/Bangkok

And please, just visit **WorldNomads.com** to check out Travel Insurance. It's better to have it and not need it; than to need it and not have it.

General Emergencies and Health

Everything from ear infections to motorbike crashes.

Emergency Clinics

 Phuket

Dr. Bangla International Clinic Patong

Open: 24/7
Where: Patong, Phuket
Address: 31 1st Floor Bangla Road - Opposite Tiger Bar, beneath Illuzion Nightclub
*Doctors will also come to your hotel if need be.
Contact: Facebook Dr. Bangla International Clinic Patong

 Bangkok

Bumrungrad Hospital Bangkok

Open: 24/7
Where: BTS Nana
Address: 33 Sukhumvit 3, Wattana, Bangkok 10110
*Considered the best hospital in Southeast Asia

 Koh Samui

Samui Home Clinic

Open: Monday-Saturday 9am-7pm
Where: Bophut
Address: 29/7, Bophut, Koh Samui

The Thailand Bucket List

- ✓ Learn How to Say 3 Words in Thai
- ✓ Drink a Coconut on the Beach
- ✓ Snorkel with Colorful Fish
- ✓ Eat a Bug or a Scorpion
- ✓ Ride in a Longtail-boat
- ✓ Take a Cooking Class
- ✓ Selfie with a Monkey
- ✓ Ride in a Songtheaw
- ✓ Visit a Night Market
- ✓ Make a Thai Friend
- ✓ Get a Thai Massage
- ✓ Visit a Thai Temple
- ✓ Eat a 7/11 Toastie
- ✓ Drink Thai Tea
- ✓ Tan Lines
- ✓ Get Lost

Behind every badass woman is a tribe of other badass women who have her back.

Coming to Thailand and have questions, want some tips or just want to chat about life in Asia?

Reach out to me on Instagram @**KohLexi**

No seriously. Message me. I'd love to hear from you and stalk your trip.

And ya'll, if you liked this book- **please leave me a review on Amazon.com!** I read every single one!!

Want to live in Thailand?
Visit HowToTeachinAsia.com

Be wild. Be safe. Message me if you need me.

from Koh Tao — Mae Haad pier

To	Dep.	Arr.
Koh Phangan	06:30 / 19:00	08:00 / 16:30
Koh Samui	06:30 / 09:00 / 15:00	08:30 / 11:00 / 17:00-17:30
Donsak	06:30 / 09:00	10:30-11:00 / 13:00-13:30
Khaosok	06:30	15:00
Surat Thani City	06:30 / 09:00	12:00 / 15:00
Surat Thani Airport	06:30 / 09:00	12:30 / 15:30
Nakhon Si Thammarat (Town)	06:30 / 09:00	12:00 / 15:00
Nakhon Si Thammarat (Airport)	06:30 / 09:00	12:30 / 15:30
Surat Thani Train Station	09:00	17:40
Krabi Town	06:30 / 09:00	14:00 / 17:00
Aonang (Krabi)	06:30 / 09:00	14:30 / 17:30
Railay Beach (Krabi)	06:30 / 09:00	14:30 / 17:30
Koh Lanta	06:30 / 09:00	17:00 / 20:00
Koh Phi Phi (Tonsai Pier)	06:30	16:30
Phuket (Rassada Pier)	06:30	17:30
Hat Yai	06:30	16:00

from Koh Phangan — Thong Sala pier

To	Dep.	Arr.
Koh Tao	08:30 / 13:30 / 17:00	10:00-10:30 / 15:00-15:30 / 18:30-19:00
Koh Samui	08:00 / 10:30 / 16:30	08:30 / 11:00 / 17:00-17:30
Donsak	08:00 / 10:30	10:30-11:00 / 13:30-13:30
Khaosok	08:00	15:00
Surat Thani City	08:00 / 10:30	12:00 / 15:00
Surat Thani Airport	08:00 / 10:30	12:30 / 15:30
Nakhon Si Thammarat (Town)	08:00 / 10:30	12:00 / 15:00
Nakhon Si Thammarat (Airport)	08:00 / 10:30	12:30 / 15:30
Surat Thani Train Station	10:30	17:40
Krabi Town	08:00 / 10:30	14:00 / 17:30
Aonang (Krabi)	08:00 / 10:30	14:30 / 17:30
Railay Beach (Krabi)	08:00 / 10:30	14:30 / 17:30
Koh Lanta	08:00 / 10:30	17:00 / 20:00
Koh Phi Phi (Tonsai Pier)	08:00	16:30
Phuket (Rassada Pier)	08:00	17:30
Hat Yai	08:00	16:00

from Koh Samui — Bangrak pier

To	Dep.	Arr.
Koh Phangan	08:00 / 13:00 / 16:30	08:30 / 13:30 / 17:00
Koh Tao	08:00 / 13:00 / 16:30	10:00-10:30 / 15:00-15:30 / 18:30-19:00
Donsak	09:00 / 11:30	10:30-11:00 / 13:00-13:30
Khaosok	09:00	15:00
Surat Thani City	09:00 / 11:30	12:00 / 15:00
Surat Thani Airport	09:00 / 11:30	12:30 / 15:30
Nakhon Si Thammarat (Town)	09:00 / 11:30	12:00 / 15:00
Nakhon Si Thammarat (Airport)	09:00 / 11:30	12:30 / 15:30
Surat Thani Train Station	11:30	17:40
Krabi Town	09:00	14:00
Aonang (Krabi)	09:00	14:30
Railay Beach (Krabi)	09:00	14:30
Koh Lanta	09:00	17:00
Koh Phi Phi (Tonsai Pier)	09:00	16:30
Phuket (Rassada Pier)	09:00	17:30
Hat Yai	09:00	16:00

from Krabi

To	Dep.	Arr.
Koh Tao	08:00 / 11:00	15:00-15:30 / 18:30-19:00
Koh Phangan	08:00 / 11:00	13:30 / 17:00
Koh Samui	08:00 / 11:00	12:30 / 16:00

from Phuket — Rassada pier

To	Dep.	Arr.
Koh Tao	08:30	18:30-19:00
Koh Phangan	08:30	17:00
Koh Samui	08:30	16:00

from Koh PhiPhi — Tonsai pier

To	Dep.	Arr.
Koh Tao	09:00	18:30-19:00
Koh Phangan	09:00	17:00
Koh Samui	09:00	16:00

*From Krabi, Phuket, and Koh Phi Phi – includes bus travel time.

Dep.= Departure time, Arr.= Arrival time

314

Printed in Great Britain
by Amazon